Write On!

The Writer's Help Book

Adrian Magson

Published by Accent Press Ltd – 2011

ISBN 9781908006776

Printed and bound in the UK

Cover design by Red Dot Design

To fellow scribes everywhere, published and
yet-to-be. Go for it.

Acknowledgements

Thanks to Liz Smith, great fiction editor, who got me this gig... and encouraged me to write more.

Thanks also to the Editor and staff of *Writing* Magazine, for allowing me the space to share my experiences

Foreword

The hardest, most challenging thing for many writers is to start writing. The next is to keep going.

This book, a collection of articles from the 'Beginners' pages of *WRITING* Magazine, is written as a source of encouragement for those new to writing ... and a reminder and lift-me-up for those of a more experienced bent. It is not a technical guide to the finer points of grammar, syntax or punctuation, but deals with the various stages of getting the words out of the wood and down on the paper, from the tentative beginning right through to THE END.

Although much of it is aimed at writing fiction, many of the disciplines, the spirit and approaches apply just as much to writing non-fiction.

I hope this book inspires, encourages, fires up, unblocks and cajoles, from hopeful start to triumphant, rampaging finish, helping scribes of all kinds to write rather than staring defeat in its dark, unwholesome face and downing their own bodyweight in black coffee, alcohol and biscuits.

AM

TABLE OF CONTENTS

Starting Out or Starting Up

THERE IS NO EASY way to start writing. You can't creep up on it stealthily and take it by surprise; nor can you sit and wait for it to happen like an attack of measles.

You just have to decide what you want to write ... then write. A bit like walking, really. Only you're leaning over a keyboard.

Breathe out. Flex the fingers ... now let the ideas flow.

Where do I begin?

I NOW KNOW HOW my father used to feel when my brother or I, on being given some information he undoubtedly thought would help us develop into mature and rounded characters, would promptly come back with, *Why's that, dad, why?* This, bear in mind, was at the tender age between *The Beano* and more 'serious' reading, where a boy's idle curiosity usually outstrips his willingness to go off and find out something for himself.

This revelatory moment came about for me after a gentleman approached me at a conference recently and announced: 'I've never written anything in my life, but I've always wanted to write a book. Trouble is, I don't know what I want to write.'

'Okaaay,' I said, not sure where this was leading. Then he hit me with the BIG one, the equivalent to the *Why, dad ...?*.

'So where do I start?'

My initial thought was that he would find it easier to knock up a nuclear power station (at least there are diagrams available for building your own version of Sellafield, and most DIY stores seem to stock everything required by a budding power freak). But, a serious question requires a proper answer – and he can't be alone in wanting to know. What I suggested is (roughly) as follows.

What's your poison? A good place to start is to consider what *you* like to read, on the basis that (a) this is the genre with which you are most familiar and (b) you should at least write something you enjoy, the alternative being, surely, madness. You might also, one hopes, have an idea of what else is on the market.

Start with a plan, Stan. Once you've decided on the genre, it helps to have a plan in mind. Will it be plot-led (say, an action thriller or a torrid romance) or character-led (a family saga, perhaps, or an individual's journey through a particular event in life – a right of passage, for example)? Is there a particular age group you're aiming at? Male or female? Adult or teens? Will it be told in the first-person or third? How many main characters will you have? What's the location – real or made up? Contemporary or historical/future setting? These are just some of the points to bear in mind, rather like deciding the shape and style of a building before you start phoning round the builders' merchants.

What's the theme? In other words, what's the main subject running through the story? Is it one of revenge? Growing up? A journey of discovery? Hardships overcome? The theme doesn't need stating outright, but recognising it might help you nail the core of the story.

Think about the structure. Ideally, every story needs a beginning, a middle and an end. No doubt some modernists will go puce and mutter 'phooey' or some such expletive to this outrageously dated suggestion, but most readers have traditional tastes, and that's who we write for, not the faddists. Knowing the structure – even in a rough form – will help you work out the rise and fall of your story, building from the introduction of your characters and setting, and leading through the progression of events to the ending. Another function of deciding the structure is to see if the story has 'legs' – in other words, do you have enough of a story to write in the first place? And will it sustain a reader's interest over, say, 80,000 words? This also comes back to the characters, because they will form an integral part of the structure. If they are not engaging, the structure falls down and your readers might as well go and read a sauce bottle.

Write a synopsis. Many writers avoid this like the plague, and only produce one on the threat of having hot needles inserted under their fingernails. But someone totally new to writing should find it a useful exercise. Bearing in mind what I said about 'legs', if you can't put enough of an idea together to write a synopsis (a synthesised version of the story), then you'll have hell's own job writing a complete one. Try writing your

4

projected story on a single sheet of paper, concentrating on hitting the main points, characters, events and the ending. From there, you can look at expanding it, adding chapter headings and outlines, secondary characters and scenes you feel are important to cover. In this way, a framework will begin to take shape – and more ideas will flow as a consequence.

Start writing. Stating the bleedin' obvious perhaps, but like walking, the best thing is to take the first step. You could try writing a short story before you attempt a novel, because then you won't have expended too much effort to see if you can do it. After that, it's a question of scale. I have to say, I've done a lot of both and find myself sweating rivets over short stories, whereas books give me far more scope and room to work in.

Either way, only when you've tried something will you know if you like it … and can actually do it. Hopefully, it will be a bit like sex: if it's good it will be great; if it's not good …well, it might still be a lot of fun.

TOP TIPS

- What do YOU like to read? What themes attract you?

- What style of writing appeals to you?

- You have to feel that you could, at least, do just as well. Better helps.

- Start with a plan. Get the ideas in your head down on paper, then flesh them out.

So what do I know?

AS NEW WRITERS WILL know, one of the most oft-repeated pieces of advice you can hear is 'write what you know'. This sometimes causes some confusion, because, on the surface, if you consider yourself to have led a fairly quiet and uneventful life, with little in the way of excitement, does it mean you don't have what it takes to write something entertaining?

Absolutely not. After all, writers of westerns or historicals can hardly travel back in time to pick up a few handy pointers, can they? And science fiction and fantasy writers can't easily travel to the other side of the universe and back, or delve into their various 'middle earths' to give them the wonderful scenes and characters about which they write with such popular approval.

However, what they do have is the ability to make up a good story, and pepper it with anything they can use from their own backgrounds or experiences to give it a real sense of atmosphere.

Thus, 'write what you know' does not mean that you must have lived a life of mayhem and excitement to create something meaningful (although it would certainly help). It means drawing on your knowledge, experience and memories, or those of other people, to build the setting and characters of your story, whatever the genre.

To help with, it pays to examine your own background for material. Because you may surprise yourself when you realise just what you have stored away in those dim, dark recesses.

Most stories are about conflict of one sort or another. And conflict arouses emotions, such as anger, fear, love, hate and so on. While few of us (if we are lucky) will have suffered the extremes of such emotions, being able to use what we have experienced can be an enormous help in our writing.

Take, for example, the very first flush of love. Remember it? Brilliant, wasn't it? Dry mouth. Wobbly knees. Guts in torment. And the vacant expression of a lovesick goldfish. Thus, if you have a scene where heroine A meets hero B, and your storyline calls for them to experience the opening flashes of love, you already have firsthand experience for this scene.

Almost by association, many who have been in love (or thought they were) will also have experienced the dreadful feeling of losing that love. (It's called being dumped, just in case you're still in denial).

But this emotion can be used in so many situations. You probably felt lost and empty? Unable to eat? Careless about your general state of well-being? That you were somewhere dark and cold, and would undoubtedly not survive the week ahead? (Even if, as it probably turned out, by Thursday you'd met someone else and all was well with the world.)

Fear is an important element in many stories, but may be more difficult to call upon. Yet you don't have to have faced a charging bull elephant to know the effects. Even a small fright can give you a dry mouth, wobbly knees (even the same vacant, goldfish expression of the love-sick). But it will be no less real and therefore useable, and can arise from all sorts of everyday events. Taking off on your first airplane flight; skiing just a little too close to the edge; that near miss on your bike; a rough swell out on open water; a dark street when you should have known better; a strange noise which wakes you in the middle of the night. How you build on these memories is up to you, but as you can see, you have the basics to begin with.

I once fell out of a sailing dinghy in the Caribbean. As the boat disappeared in the general direction of South America, and I began to realise how vulnerable I was in that vast mass of water, I consoled myself with the thought that I was wearing a lifejacket and I could swim. Then something solid and heavy brushed against my leg. Scared? Me? I should cocoa. There are parts of me that still shrivel up at the memory ... but one day I'll use that experience to good effect.

On a more mundane level, have you ever stepped off a pavement into traffic? You either stepped back smartly, horribly embarrassed, or jumped back, thanking your lucky stars for your ninja-like reflexes. Either way, you probably found your thoughts jumbled for a while afterwards, contemplating what *might* have happened if you hadn't ...

Remember it, picture it, feel the emotions all over again, then write them down. They don't need to be elaborately detailed – your story may only call for a brief rush of a similar feeling – but they will be authentic, because they come from within you.

Any event in your life which symbolises a successful outcome can bring on a whole range of powerful emotions. They might be variously described as relief, joy, euphoria, satisfaction, achievement ... or simply the pleasure of proving to someone that you could do something. But if you can recall those feelings at the time (passing an exam, a driving test, scoring a goal, achieving that hole-in-one), you will be able to describe more realistically the feelings relating to, say, your hero or heroine achieving something difficult in another sphere.

TOP TIPS

- Look at your own life experiences – you might be surprised by what you have stored away in your mind.

- Recall moments of real emotion – love, loss, joy, disappointment or fear – and use them to describe emotion in your characters.

- Remembering the physical characteristics caused by these emotions – heightened breathing, dry lips, increased or lowered energy levels – all these can help bring realism to your writing.

- Writing what you know is more often writing what you know *about*.

So what *else* do I know?

THE ALTERNATIVE TO BEING able to draw on personal experience, whereby we delve into our own memory banks for detail is, quite simply, to poach from others. We can't, after all, have done many of the things we might choose to write about, especially in the field of crime or thriller writing, or where the story has a specific setting beyond our reach. But, as writers, we should try to ensure that where something is verifiable, we are as accurate as possible. This can best be described as using the 'I don't know, but I know a man who does' approach.

As an example of this, witness the lengthy list of 'credits' at the beginning of some novels – especially in the US, where everybody including Billy-Bob and his uncle seems to get a mention. Some of these authors must have bugged the life out of countless people and organisations in their desire to achieve a sense of authenticity.

Now, while a few fortunate writers may have professional access through a former job to all kinds of useful people to whom they can go for some inside knowledge (journalists, for example), most of us have to depend on acquaintances, friends, family, other experts – basically, anyone we can blag into disclosing whatever details we need to give flesh to our stories.

Jargon. Probably the most common example where this applies is in the field of **policing**, where in order to get a sense of accuracy about language, methodology and procedure, a friendly policeman or the local constabulary press office are the best sources of information. Indeed, some well-known authors have, in their search for realism, built close relationships with serving officers, in order to gain insights into a world that is not open to the average punter. (Not that I'm suggesting you all dash out there and do likewise; hoards of eager writers scouring pubs and bars for off-duty coppers would hardly help police-community relations!)

The **military** world is another, possessing its own language and, like the police, with its own outlook on the rest of the world. Seeing life through a soldier's eyes is something that can rarely be imagined unless you have been in the army, and writing a story with an army, navy or air force background is fraught with problems purely on the question of technology alone; throw in things like command structures, terminology, slang, etiquette and culture, each of which is different for the different services, and your 'outsider' status will show up immediately to those in the know if you haven't done your research.

The **medical** profession is another common setting for stories, where the level of detail required to flesh out the atmosphere and practices might be beyond the immediate scope of many writers.

However, none of these obstacles should prevent writers from tackling the subject matter. What you have to do is decide on the level at which you want to pitch your story, and how detailed it needs to be. Once you have decided that, find a source for the amount of information you need, be it serving or past members of the specific field, or any branch that will give you access to the data required.

Surprisingly, a lot of our research – especially of a general nature – might begin much closer to home. What if you are writing with a historical bent – say, about the period from the First World War on? The detail here will need to be accurate, because it will be within the memory of people still living, and therefore open to judgement by readers. What better way to cover all the bases than by talking to some of those people in order to get the detail just right?

Fortunately, there are still many of the older generation around with photo albums to back up what you need, and often only too willing to talk about that time. You might not need much; just sufficient to give your scenes that definite touch of authenticity that will come across to the reader.

And this touches on the question of lives lived, yet all too rarely spoken of. Even among families, there are members – especially those of an advanced age – who have lived through some startling events and packed more into their lives than their younger relatives can begin to imagine. Yet they might never have talked about their experiences. In particular, anyone who has lived through the wars, or worked in difficult areas overseas, for example, may see no reason why they should talk about what to them is merely history. Yet they are an invaluable source of information, observers of historical developments large and small, with specific emotions, opinions and a whole wealth of other detail reeking of authenticity.

One thing to be wary of, however, is trying to provide too much information. Your story is first and foremost an entertainment, and should not become bogged down by unnecessary facts, or overburdened with so much description it detracts from the plot. If you don't need to mention how many buttons a soldier has on his uniform, or the number of a police report after an arrest, then don't.

As to the rest … well, you might just have to make it up.

TOP TIPS

- If you need to know how someone does their job – ask him, or her.

- Consider family members, who may have experience or knowledge of the type you need.

- Every profession has its own jargon and language.

- Get it right – you owe it to your readers.

Write outside the square

I WAS ASKED RECENTLY at a literary bash what sort of writing I did. When I explained that I wrote various things, ranging from articles to short stories to books – even radio comedy material for a while – I received the kind of look you get when you accidentally step on someone's freshly seeded lawn.

It seemed I had somehow transgressed in the other person's eyes, as if engaging in more than one kind of writing was abnormal. My interlocutor, incidentally, claimed to write 'only serious material', without revealing quite what that was.

However, it set me thinking. What he clearly found so odd was that I couldn't be slotted into a convenient box marked 'Short Story Writer', 'Poet', 'Feature Writer', or whatever. And it's not the first time I've encountered this reaction.

Unless you like to work in a specific field, I don't see what's wrong with ploughing a broad furrow. You may possess background knowledge or experience which allows you to concentrate on a particular subject area, which is fine. But most writers I know inevitably try a variety of subjects or styles along the way, whether by accident, design or commission (the latter being where you get to eat once in a while).

Trying things out. Merely another way of flexing your **writing muscles**, and on the simple basis that you never know what you can do until you try, there's a good argument for it.

Of course, the act of putting words on paper is common to all writing, but there are some basic differences in the pursuit and practice between, say, writing a piece of fiction and penning a magazine article. But they're hardly insurmountable.

Fiction gives you complete freedom to write what you wish. It's your world, so as long as your characters, setting and events are believable and acceptable to your target market, anything goes. And most, if not all, your creativity can take place at your desk, the main tools being your mind and whatever information sources you might have at hand.

Non-fiction requires a slightly different approach, where accuracy is essential if you want to gain and maintain credibility. Fail to state the correct facts (and there's *always* somebody out there who knows) and your writing will be questioned, usually with fatal results for any future projects. Accumulating these facts requires physical study, interviews or research into the subject in libraries, museums or on the Internet.

However, we're only varying our working practice slightly, not re-inventing the wheel, and we try other forms of activity in life, so why not with writing?

Sport, for example. Most of us grow up playing one or more forms of sport, be it football, hockey, swimming, etc. Most of our choices are governed by background, education or simply the facilities available. But just because we've always kicked a ball about, doesn't mean it's the *only* thing we should do.

Many of us in this country rarely see snow from one year's end to the next (even as I write this, I've a feeling I may regret it). But if we're lucky enough to try winter sports on holiday, we may discover an ability to ski with reasonable, even consummate, ease. Some of us who rarely go near water except to wash, find we have a real and hitherto untapped affinity with the stuff when given a wetsuit, flippers and sub-aqua equipment (OK, and tropical temperatures to go with them!)

Both sports may be very different forms of activity from our personal norm, yet we're still using the same basic equipment, albeit with the add-on of curved planks or floppy shoes to help us along a bit.

Similarly, writing is writing, whatever you are working on. And until you test yourself, you may be unaware that you have the ability to do something you'd never considered before.

Marshalling facts for a feature is excellent training for developing a control of detail in a work of fiction. If your story is set in a real, identifiable town, for example, it helps to ensure your description of roads, places and the general layout is as accurate as possible, otherwise it will be spoiled for people who know the place you're writing about.

Creating scenes from nothing is essential when writing non-fiction. The topic may be factual, even dry, but it still needs to be an entertaining read. And the creative use of words you employ in writing fiction can help you lift the page from being a listing of facts and figures into something enjoyable.

So, unless you wish to stick rigidly to one genre, it might pay to consider others. Changing projects every now and then is a useful way of refreshing your work and giving yourself a break. And writing something outside your normal comfort zone might help spread your talents to other, equally rewarding fields.

More than anything, though, next time anyone asks what you do, you can tell them quite simply and positively.

You're a writer. End of story.

TOP TIPS

- Trying different writing styles is like flexing different muscles.

- You already possess the equipment – just use it for different tasks.

- Refuse to be pigeonholed.

- You never know what you can do until you try.

Fact or fiction … or both?

I WAS ONCE NAIVE enough to mention to a musician friend that I had always wanted to play the guitar. 'Really?' he said. 'What sort?' He then went on to list, among others, rock, classical, Spanish, lead, bass and Country & Western. This signalled the end of the conversation and a silent promise never to be so vague again.

But my string-picking pal had a point. How could I want to do something without at least some idea of the field involved?

Many years ago, markets for writers were pretty much restricted to fiction or journalism. That many successful authors today actually learned their craft writing for regional or national newspapers highlights the fact that journalism was – and, for some, still is – the starting point in their careers.

But over recent years the publishing world has changed dramatically. With the increase in magazines, and the Internet revolution, the choices and market opportunities for writers have expanded hugely. However, one question still remains: Do I write fiction or non-fiction?

Well, why not aim to do both?

Some writers find the idea of crossing between fiction and features difficult. This may be a matter of comfort, or because they have specialised knowledge which fuels their focus as a writer. A background in commerce, for example, may give ample scope for writing about corporate or financial matters, without the need or desire to expand into other areas. Similarly, a background in the police may anchor a writer happily in the crime genre.

But the fact is, given the ability and the desire to write, there are arguments for trying your hand at more than one genre. And whether producing a feature on corporate training or a short story with a thriller/crime bent, it involves sticking to some fairly basic – and surprisingly similar – rules:

- **Market**. You need a buyer for your work. No market means no sale.

- **Imagination.** Producing a fresh, saleable feature requires as much imagination as does a piece of fiction. Putting facts on paper is simple; making them interesting enough for someone to read and enjoy requires something extra.

- **Structure**. All writing needs a structure on which to build. With luck, most stories have a beginning, a middle and an end (although not always, according to some examples). But features, too, need to start somewhere, take the reader through the body (middle) of the piece and, obviously, come to some sort of conclusion or wrap.

- **Tell a story.** Even a piece on running, say, a successful marketing department, should ideally tell a story, rather than being a simple presentation of facts. Using anecdotes or dialogue (interviews) in a feature introduces a sense of reality to an otherwise bland collection of paragraphs. As an example, take any feature in a magazine, and ten to one the piece sprinkled with interviews, comments and anecdotes will attract your interest, rather than the heavy paragraphs with few or no breaks to relieve the layout.

- **Information.** Writing should inform; characters, settings and plot in a story, and subject matter, facts and details, etc., in a feature. Both need to grip the readers' attention, either by subject or originality, otherwise their interest won't last – and they certainly won't come back for more.

- **Entertainment**. As with stories, the ideal feature should leave the reader feeling satisfied or surprised. There's a huge number of special interest magazines purchased every week (cars, pets, activities, collectibles, etc.), yet many of the readers have little or no hands-on contact with the actual subject matter. They simply enjoy reading about them.

- **Planning.** Essential to any writing, you need to plan ahead. This includes studying the target market, story length, viewpoint, style, content and, with seasonal material, the calendar. (Most magazines work at least three months in advance, often longer.)

- **Getting It Right.** A feature giving incorrect data will either not get past the editor or will soon lose a well-informed reader's interest. Equally, get your facts wrong in a short story, such as the distance from A to B or the procedure in a criminal investigation, and someone out there will let you know!

There are, of course, some differences between the two types of writing. Features often require photos or info-boxes to support the content, or bullet points to highlight certain paragraphs. Fiction does not. It does, however – especially with SF or Fantasy writing – allow your imagination to soar to heights limited only by the editor's pen.

While fiction engages the use of emotion, humour, drama and invention, features generally require a more ordered approach to facts and presentation, and a more formal language and style. Breaks within a feature allow readers to pause between segments, whereas in short (magazine) fiction they are rare. In today's busy world, many readers will absorb a feature in bite-sized chunks, while a short story is mostly absorbed in one sitting.

So why should I try both?

Why not? Broadening your scope will increase your market and saleability as a writer. And when you find yourself going through a sticky patch in one, switching to another is a useful way of clearing that blockage rather than taking a long hike, eating your body-weight in biscuits or kicking your PC through the nearest window.

TOP TIPS

- Decide about what you want to write.

- Consider what might be required in terms of commitment, time and effort.

- Learn the rules and guidelines. It could make the difference between success or failure.

- Consider the market opportunities and rewards.

Writing fit

NOT LONG AFTER MAKING the jump from writing intermittently
– which, for me was at weekends and some evenings – to
pounding a keyboard full-time, I began to feel some aches and
pains coming on. Nothing too obvious at first; a twinge here
and there, an ache in my arms which I put down to coinciding
with discovering my first pale hair (the concept of the colour
grey being alien at the time). But within a couple of weeks I
was beginning to feel as if I'd gone a couple of rounds in an
arm-wrestling contest – and lost.

I ignored it, of course, being a square-jawed type of guy, and
put it down to the last bout of decorating. But pretty soon even I
couldn't ignore it, and spoke to my brother-in-law, a
chiropractor. His diagnosis? I'd changed my working practice
(zipping around Europe, hopping on and off planes and in and
out of cars, all very active) to sitting at home slowly melting
into my chair. In short, my body was trying to adjust to new
habits and postures but I wasn't helping by trying to be Super
Writer.

Now this may be stating the bleedin' obvious, but if you
took up swimming, and had the habit of breathing in when you
should be breathing out, would you ignore it? Not a great
analogy, I know … but I believe that anything which gets in the
way of pursuing your interest – in this case, writing – should be
taken seriously.

Re-wind many years to when I didn't have a spare room in
which to do my writing. Huddled in a draughty bedsit, I would
scribble sitting cross-legged on the bed or in my moth-eaten,
fifth-hand armchair. Even years later when I had a kitchen table
and a spare room, sitting on a hard chair all weekend was no

problem; my body could cope and adjust.

However, writing then was not my full-time work, and I was a lot younger. Change both facts and you find there are adjustments to make – even if only writing part-time. In addition, nobody said suffering for your art was obligatory.

Posture. Whether you use a PC or note paper, you need to sit correctly, which means not slumped, not leaning at a perilous angle over a low table, and not twisted sideways like a teenager doing homework. If you work at a small table, and have a large monitor which has to be set at an angle to fit, you probably sit with your head skewed to one side. This will soon make itself felt on your shoulders and neck. If you can, invest in a flat screen and work head-on. This will help your posture and stop you twisting your body at an unnatural angle.

Comfort. Avoid sharp edges digging into the forearms or wrists. Over a long period, this can be painful, as well as producing a tingling feeling which will hamper concentration and enjoyment. If using a keyboard, adjust your chair to the height of the table or desk and, if you need to, cushion the wrists by use of a foam rest.

Lighting needs to be adequate, especially if your writing is done in the evening or in a small room. Sitting in poor light and squinting at the screen will produce tired eyes, if not a pounding headache. Sitting too close to the screen will do the same.

Breaks. Downing tools may seem counter-productive when in full writerly flow, but even a quick walk around the room and some upper-body stretching is better than nothing. If you can, go for a stroll and get some fresh air; stuck in a stuffy room, the brain can soon slip into hibernation mode without us noticing, which does nothing at all for our creative juices. By sticking at it like the boy on the burning deck when all your senses are telling you to give it a break, you are doing yourself a disservice, potentially ruining your chances of success.

Refreshments. Dehydration is another danger for the heads-down writer. You need regular liquid intake or your body will start to notice. Pretty soon you may develop a muzzy head and lose concentration. Personally, I don't subscribe to the two litres a day rule (I tried it once and nearly had to set up my writing position in the bathroom, I was spending so much time in there), but I do take regular drink breaks because I notice the difference in performance when I don't.

Down-time. Burning the midnight oil sounds so romantic, doesn't it? Slogging away in utter peace at your latest work while everyone else is sleeping can produce a real blast of concentration. I know because I still do it from time to time, when I need to get something down on paper before I lose the idea altogether. But you have to listen to your body and not push it too far. Otherwise, before you know it, that brilliant burst of creativity has been torpedoed by the last hundred words, which were added long after you should have called it a night.

TOP TIPS

- Don't let bad posture spoil your writing. Sit comfortably and write well.

- Poor light will not help your creative bursts – or your eyesight.

- Take regular breaks to keep body and mind fresh.

- Suffering for one's art is not part of the job description!

Planning your novel (Pt 1)

NOW SEEMS LIKE A good time to mention my father and his various quirks. One that occurred to me recently was his passion for planning car journeys. OK, so where's this going?

Stick with me; it's a tenuous link, I admit, but relevant.

Father's approach to planning involved many cups of tea and more maps than Montgomery's North Africa campaign. And took about the same amount of time. Actually, trotting across the desert would have been child's play to him, because he'd done it for real, back when men used Brylcreem instead of gel and wore giant shorts made of canvas with regulation creases down the front.

Whatever the trip, he planned numerous rest stops, with places of interest to visit *en route*. Not that they were of much interest to the rest of us, but that's another story. Essential to this were lay-bys to park in to fire up the portable stove for a brew, complete with camping chairs – a matter of toe-curling embarrassment for my brother and me. He also planned locations for emergency overnight stops – nearly always in a field with a slope just to keep us on out toes throughout the night. He was very good that way.

But he always got us there and back, because he worked to a plan.

This degree of forethought has often come back to me when working on a novel (see the link?) because embarking on a book is much like taking a journey. You don't always know where it will lead, and circumstances might force a change of direction along the way … but at least you should avoid too many wrong turnings and ending up in somebody's prize manure heap. It therefore makes sense to plan before you leave.

If you don't, as my old man was wont to say, you could end up going round and round and vanishing up your own fundament.

In short, planning helps you explore the possibilities in your writing and maximise the potential of a storyline … and deal with some of the pitfalls you might encounter along the way.

There are, of course, authors who do not plan. They simply sit down and write, the words pouring forth in a fair old gush of consciousness. Lucky them. On the other hand, none of us knows how long they've been thinking about it.

So how to plan? Well, there are various methods and levels to use, among them the following:

1. Rough sketch. Anything from back-of-an-envelope scratchings to a casual list of how you see the story going. This is planning at its most basic – but can lead on to so much more if it opens up the thinking process.

2. Book synopsis. A more orderly storyline 'telling' the story in brief detail so you can follow a more-or-less pre-determined path. This kind of synopsis would be used in the same way when approaching agents or publishers, but, one hopes, a 'cleaned up' version complete with the characters and – most importantly – the ending.

3. Chapter synopsis. This calls for greater detail showing the progression by chapter, but presumes a greater focus on sticking tightly to the storyline. This way, each chapter becomes almost a mini-book, showing the beginning, middle, and end.

4. Key point indicator. Taking up from the rough sketch, this method might be useful, for example, when planning a thriller, showing the main bursts of action and tension which would form the backbone of your plot. You still have to fill in all the gaps in between, but this offers a useful framework to start with.

5. Diary plan. The timeline – the chronology of events in the correct order – is often the most difficult bit to get right. Creating a diary (whether the story takes place over an hour or several days/weeks, it doesn't matter) is essential for keeping everything in the right order, so that you don't find events tripping over each other, or characters out of position. This method is particularly useful when the timing and duration of events is crucial to the story, especially when taking place over a very tight time-span, where every second or minute counts.

6. Character biographies. This can be anything from a couple of lines of description to a full biography, showing background, age, family, education, jobs, relationships and so forth. If your story is character-led, knowing how they might react according to type is vital. It ensures you keep the physical characteristics constant, too. Cutting out a photo of someone resembling each of your characters is a useful way of doing this and keeps the faces fresh in your memory.

7. Theme? Could you describe your book in one sentence (the **elevator pitch** of film fame)? Settling on the basic story and theme in easily described shorthand might help put it into perspective, even in your own mind.

Even given my father's benign, Monty-esque influence, I prefer a mix of 1 and 4, with a dash of 5. But that's just me. Whatever *your* choice of method, each can contribute in its own subtle way to the planning process, because together they can help you maintain control and focus on where the book is going.

TOP TIPS

- Planning helps clarify direction and method.

- Having a plan helps you focus and saves time and effort.

- A plan will show you the possibilities, potential and pitfalls in your story.

- Good planning means you already have some of the work done before you begin writing.

Planning your novel (Pt 2)

FOLLOWING ON FROM THE last chapter, other aspects of planning your novel might fall under the rather pedestrian heading of 'product research'.

- What is your **target market**? (If you don't know, your intended publisher might not, either). Having an audience in mind will help you during the writing process.

- What's the **competition**? What work might it be compared to?

- What is the approximate **word count** and will it match similar titles?

- **Chapter length**. The fashion is now for shorter chapters, useful for increasing tension and making for a faster pace of narrative. Again, check the competition.

- Has it got the legs to be a book, or is it merely a short story with lofty pretensions?

- **Location** – real or made up? If it's a real place, get to know it and get it right. If made up, it can help to 'borrow' a mix of genuine locations and scenery to add texture and colour.

- **Setting** – contemporary, historical or future? The detail must be convincing (perhaps with the exception of 'future' works), as the backdrop descriptions serve to identify time, place and atmosphere.

- **Viewpoint.** First person allows a single point of view only (you are in your storyteller's mind all the way). Third person allows other points of view and broader scope.

Some books have both, alternating between the two, but this needs treating with skill to avoid confusing the reader.

- **Character names**. Ideally, these should match the period, location and even the age or class of the characters. A mismatch can cause the reader to stumble, chipping away at their enjoyment.

Other points which may impact on your writing:

The title. Has it been used before (recently), and could yours cause confusion to the reader/buyer? An impulsive click on an online site can be an easy mistake for a reader if two similar titles are close together, and disappointing for the author, for whom every sale counts in numbers and royalties. An additional reason for having a title you like is because it allows you to feel that this is yours and nobody else's. Try getting passionate about 'My Next Book'. Doesn't quite work, does it?

Series or stand-alone. What if, heavens to Betsy, an interested publisher asks for a second book with the same characters? Readers love series, and for you this can lead to follow-up sales and the likelihood of a prolonged career. It would also involve some fundamental decisions about your writing output and forward planning, as a series calls for longevity of characters and an ever-growing biography – as well as plans for their future. And producing a number of stand-alones requires a constant supply of fresh ideas, each having to be built from new. It has been said that a succession of individual novels is like a bus journey; the vehicle stays the same but the passengers must change.

Direction and outcome. Ultimately, this is about where your story – and the readers – are going. You have to decide:

- Is the journey emotional, physical or psychological – and where will it take them?

- How? Will it be through action, drama or trial and tribulation?

- Who is involved? (The good, the bad and the in-betweens).

- What obstacles will they meet along the way? High points: love, danger, thrills. Low points: loss, uncertainty and disappointment.

- In most stories, the main characters have to change in some way. Something must happen to them, so that the reader can follow their development.

Research. Becoming bogged down in the detail is a real danger, but in order to get things right, you have to consider all avenues and how far you want to go. (At least with an excess of research, you might end up with enough material for another book!)

- **Internet.** Fast, vast and efficient, but too much late-night on-screen activity can lead to eye strain, pale skin and a tendency for neighbours to view you with suspicion.

- **Bookshops**. Whether testing the market by studying similar books or gathering background information, getting close to the look and smell of the market place is a great motivator – you just can't wait to be part of it.

- **Visiting real places.** Much more fun – and healthier – but time-consuming.

- **Newspapers/archives**. If your book is fact-based, or you need historical detail, you might need to consult facilities like the British Library archives in Colindale, north London. (Check availability after 2012.)

- **Real People.** If you know anyone with expertise or knowledge useful to your novel, it is worth plumbing this valuable resource. It's always a surprise to find just how much people love talking about their jobs and experiences.

- **How** and **When**. Do you research before you start writing, as you go, or after the first draft? The plain answer is, whichever suits you best. Deciding on the how and when before you begin will help you make the best use of your time and resources.

All that's left now is to decide when to begin the actual writing – now or later?

I jest. There's never a later.

Start now.

TOP TIPS

- Think about the 'look' of your book and its physical characteristics.

- Plan the research as well as the story. One will undoubtedly impact on the other.

- Consider future writing plans and how the current project might affect them.

- If you have a clear idea about your book, it will make the writing so much easier.

Get on with it!

IT'S A SAFE BET, even without publishing industry figures, that over the summer holidays, book and magazine sales will probably be healthier than at any time of the year other than Christmas. After all, summer is a time for relaxing, isn't it? For putting your feet up and doing the things you don't normally have time to do. And whether stretched out on a beach somewhere, or enjoying the gentle, skin-caressing softness of British rain (that's a bit of spin, not poetry) or revelling in the peace and quiet of a cottage in the back of beyond, catching up on leisure reading is a brilliant way of sloughing off all those problems which beset us throughout the rest of the year.

But hold on just a cotton-picking minute. *Reading?* We're writers, aren't we? And haven't we been promising ourselves for months now that when we do get some time off, we'll settle down and start that story/book/play we've always wanted to write if only we had time and A BIT OF PEACE AND QUIET?

Of course we have. And whether you're a fresh-skinned beginner with the writing bug, or a professional with calluses where your fingertips used to be, the urge to write never, ever quite goes away. Which means, naturally, that the holiday period and the weeks after will be a prime time for getting that piece of writing started.

OK. So how do you go about starting?

Well, I'm not saying abandon all those hoarded best sellers and grind away for two weeks over a hot notebook. That's not what it's about. Forced writing generally leads to forced results, which is never satisfactory. And as most writers will tell you, a good way of getting the creative juices flowing is to read as much as you can. Like every other aspect of life, you need some balance.

Firstly, the most basic piece of holiday equipment is not sun lotion, flips-flops or a corkscrew; it's a pen and paper. As a writer, I always try to have the basic tools with me at all times. So does every other writer I know, which explains why so many of us have larger-than-average pockets. Unfortunately, being of a normal, vague mind, I occasionally forget – which usually coincides with a flash of inspiration and has me scrabbling for something with which to write it down before it vanishes into the ether.

The good old envelope and stubby pencil are the entry-level requirements, or you can be really flash and go for the latest in laptop technology. But let's be reasonable, a decent notebook and ballpoint will do – until, of course, you land that massive, three-book deal with a mega advance …

So now you need some inspiration. Well, unless you take your holidays on a different planet to me, you'll have already spotted more characters, scenes and potential plots on the first day than you can shake a plastic bucket at.

Take that strange man on the beach (and I don't mean your husband). Who is he? What does he do for a living? Could he be there for reasons other than a simple paddle in the sea? Is he a cheat, hero, rogue or saint? Could that woman alongside him be someone other than, say, his normal partner?

Out of this gentle musing, you can weave your story, safely hidden behind dark glasses and building fantasy scenes and characters out of real places and people.

That old house down the lane from where you're staying. Does it have an aura suggesting a dark secret? What could have happened there – possibly to do with the local area or history? Could you build a story out of the bricks and mortar, peopled with your own set of heroes and villains?

And that young couple staring adoringly at each other in the corner of the room. How did they get to this point? Are they in the first flush of a new relationship, or could one of them be harbouring a secret desire to be miles away, preferably staring with even more adoration at somebody else?

Such scenes, characters and possibilities are all around us. But most flash by without registering, our attention too taken up with everyday matters to take note.

Yet here is the ideal opportunity; the opportunity we've been *promising* ourselves for however long. We're on holiday, we're relaxed, we're receptive to ideas, we have little or no agenda to worry about and the talking has gone on long enough.

So, assuming you've made lots of notes, begun the first few paragraphs or fleshed out the synopsis of a novel, you're now entering that time of year when you had also promised yourself an evening class or two, to learn a useful skill.

What better time to join a writing group or writing classes, to keep the momentum and juices going before it all filters away into the soft soil of everyday life?

As John Wayne might have said: *Get off your horse and drink your milk!*

Or, more prosaically (if slightly ungrammatically), you'll only ever *be* a writer if you *do* writing.

TOP TIPS

- The best time to write is when you're relaxed and free of worries about work.

- Don't ignore the writing possibilities in scenes and events all around you.

- Allow your creative juices to float free and conjure up whatever comes to mind.

- If you really want to be a writer – then write.

Keeping It Going

THE ACT OF WRITING is a bit like pushing a car; you have to keep going or you'll soon slow down and stop. The more you write, the more ideas will come to you, and the more the discipline of writing will take over.

It's a bit like sex. The more you enjoy it, the better you will become.

Only pushing a car is nowhere near as much fun ...

So what have *you* done today …?

THIS MAY HAVE SOME writers throwing a blue wobbly, but I have to confess to a secret: I *don't* write every single day. Well, I have a life to lead, too, and life has a habit of getting in the way sometimes. Take last week, for instance, when I put my foot through the ceiling while insulating the loft. Or maybe that's best forgotten …

But, while I might not be actually writing (and here I'll paraphrase comedian Terry Scott in that song about his brother), you don't know what I'm thinking about, do you? As my wife can testify, repeated calls from Earth to Planet Adrian often fail to penetrate the muggy wool of creative thought, no matter what I'm up to.

It's said that every journey begins with the first step. Unfortunately, many journeys – in a writing sense, at least – never take place. Why? Because many writers never actually get round to doing what they're dreaming of, which is writing.

'If only I had time …' is one of the most repeated complaints one hears from would-be writers (and readers, sadly, which is quite scary), and nobody is doubting the relentless pull of work, family, relationships, DIY, chat-room, mobile phone and so on.

But who said you had to write a whole book in one sitting? Do you eat a whole year's supply of food in one go? Do you paint the entire house in one day (especially when having to extricate your foot from the ceiling)?

I know setting goals can be boring, and I wouldn't suggest anyone regiments their life to the extent that they constantly have their eyes on some kind of daily writing routine. That can stifle creativity faster than a dose of migraine, and we all have enough routines to choke an elephant. But looking at a way of getting round that flurry of everyday activity which kills off any attempt at writing, it can be done realistically, if you have the willpower and desire.

A gentleman recently told me with absolute conviction, 'I never have a minute to write – I only wish I did.' He then went on to list all the things he had to do every day, which kept him on his feet and unable to pursue his love of writing. My suggestion was to use his time in the bathroom to greater effect.

I'm not sure he was too impressed by this. But if he really was as hectically busy as he implied, surely he owed it to himself to snatch at least a few minutes with a notepad – no matter where? If a man's home really is his castle, then his bathroom must be not only the smallest, but the most private room in the house.

Conversely, a lady in a bookshop had a completely different attitude. She told me that whenever she managed to write something, no matter how brief, she felt a huge sense of achievement, even pride. She was also very busy, but managed to find and use little pockets in her day to good effect, even if it meant writing just the first line of a new story or sketching out a fresh scene which had suddenly occurred to her.

She was, quite simply, doing it rather than merely thinking about it.

Ceilings notwithstanding, I do this myself, even when I'm working on other projects. I jot down ideas, take snatches of dialogue which sound appealing, and I constantly think about what I'm currently working on or would like to work on next. In fact, if I were to check my IDEAS folder, I'd find stuff which will probably take me years to get round to … or maybe just a couple of days, because in there might be something that will fit in with a project I'm currently writing.

I liken it to chipping away at a large chunk of wood; eventually, I'll have something recognisable which I can work on more fully and with more energy and focus, because the *desire* to do it will push me to get on with it.

And that's the key: if you want to do something enough, you will manage it somehow. If you have that inner burn to write, that itch that won't go away, especially when you pick up a good book or a short story and think you could do just as well, you will find a way. It may be a sentence here or a short piece of dialogue there; it might even be thinking of a name for a character, or a description. But those small, even minute achievements are not to be dismissed lightly. Because they will add up, and they will grow, as will your determination to make something of them, no matter how busy. And that's a greater achievement.

TOP TIPS

- Snatch those pockets in your life (travelling, queuing, waiting – and yes, in the bathroom) to write *something*.

- Thought of a scene? Sketch it out in six words – you can write it out later.

- Give yourself the pleasure of having started something – but don't let it stop there.

- Say 'I'm writing' – and mean it.

- Go to sleep with a sense of achievement.

Keeping It Going (continued)

You need momentum

IF YOU'VE EVER TRIED push-starting a car, you'll know from experience – and the pitiful grunting noises you make – that once you've got the vehicle moving, it's a lot easier to keep it going. Meet a bump along the way and let the momentum slacken off even just a bit, and you'll find getting it going again is a whole lot harder.

Similarly – and this applies to beginners and professionals, writing fiction or non-fiction – the activity of writing can succeed or suffer by the use of – or lack of – momentum.

Although not quite as energy-sapping as pushing a car (writing is surprisingly physical – ask any writer about back or shoulder problems) the mental element needs forward motion, too. And like pushing the car, the moment that forward motion drops off, whether caused by the demands of family life, work pressures, sickness, friends, tiredness, despondency or the simple blank page, getting the creative juices flowing again once we've stopped can be really tough.

I tend to think of this momentum as a form of electricity. You'll know what I mean if you've ever had that buzz in your stomach about a particular passage you were writing, or a scene you were constructing. The details seem to leap vividly on to the paper in front of you without too much effort or thought, the pictures or words crowding in and demanding to be put down before the pen runs out, the lights go off or the keyboard begins to smoulder and the neighbours start pounding on the wall because it's two in the morning.

That's what happens when momentum is working for you. And it's best to take full advantage when it comes along. (And don't worry too much about grammar or punctuation – the main aim is to get that torrent of words down while it's pouring forth.

The tidying up – editing – can come later!)

The exciting thing for any writer is that momentum like this can fizz away quite happily, carrying us forward at such a rate that time itself seems unimportant. OK, it's tough on those around us when they can't get past the thousand-yard stare of creative concentration, but the understanding ones soon learn to adapt!

When I get these moments, I have been known to forget time, sleeping or eating – and once, even getting off a train at the right stop – or the fact that the extremely patient and understanding lady in the next room would really quite like me to pop my head round the door and say 'hi' once in a while!

Naturally, it's not possible to harness this momentum all the time. But there are ways of getting it working for you, and most of them are a combination of factors, connected with both the words you're putting on paper and the act of writing itself.

- Is something interesting happening to your story, or does it feel as if it's wallowing, like a tired old boat on a sluggish river? If honestly the latter, make something happen. As one famous writer once said: 'Kill someone!' (On paper, of course).

- Can you honestly say your characters are going on some kind of journey? This can be physical or emotional, but there should be some movement in such a way that they are not standing still and beginning to fade into the background.

- Are you eager to get on with what you are writing, and can't wait to get back to the desk/table/spare room/garden shed? If not, it probably means you should reflect on what you've done so far, and decide where your idea is going.

- Do aspects of your story make you smile, make you excited or set your heart beating in any way? Do you feel any emotion at all for the characters or their situation? If the whole thing leaves you cold, and you don't have a 'connection' with your subject, then it probably won't do much for the reader, either.

- At the end of each writing stint, whether the luxury of a whole day or a snatch of precious time in between other activities, do you have a plan for the next session? Do you have a to-do list so you can pick up where you left off? Do you find you have a pile of jottings about characters, scenes, direction, corrections and other editing tasks you want to do? If not, you should get into the habit. Because these help keep up that momentum, keeping you focussed and intent on not letting that precious forward motion drain away.

When you've finished the story or article, do you submit it and get on with the next piece or sit back and wait for the reaction? If the latter, you'll immediately lose momentum and fall into 'dead ground', too concerned with mugging the postman every morning to keep up the creative flow. Far better to log it, forget about it and get on with something else.

There are no hard and fast figures for how many different pieces you should have out there at any one time, but more than one is a good start! And if a piece does come back with a rejection, *send it out to someone else!* That 'no thanks' is only one person's opinion, remember, there are many more out there.

TOP TIPS

- Don't allow your interest in what you are writing to flag. Keep moving forward.

- Get back to your writing as soon as you can, to ensure momentum.

- Keep thinking of the next scene, chapter – or even the next project.

- When you've finished one project, send it off and begin the next.

Keeping It Going (continued)

Poetry in motion

THERE'S A TEMPTATION – ONE to which I've succumbed on more than one occasion – to keep locations simple by setting the story in one place. It cuts down on the need for new descriptive narrative every couple of pages, does away with describing the waiter, passer-by, cop, cat or motorcar in the background and allows one to concentrate on the action and main characters. Rather like watching a play with a single stage setting.

I once wrote a short story about two people stuck in a lift together – and you don't get much more singular or sparse in setting than that.

However, if we think about reality for a moment, our daily lives are rarely spent in the same place – certainly not in the same room – so it makes sense to vary the setting in our stories whenever we can, to give a sense of verisimilitude, as well as giving us a fresh diversion.

In my lift story, it was by default, entirely emotion-led. The two characters in this conked-out Otis were two older work colleagues, who had co-existed fairly amicably for years, but weren't about to hurl themselves around the place in fits of passion just because they could (there wasn't room, anyway). Once resigned to their temporary fate, they were destined by my storyline to talk themselves into a greater understanding – and yes, I admit, there was a touch of budding romance involved as a result, since it transpired that they had admired each other from afar across the filing trays, but constraints of one sort or another had prevented them doing anything about it. (I know, the words *kiss, you morons!* hangs in the air).

OK, it might sound cheesy, but the market I was writing for at the time wanted a heart-warming story of a gentler kind, not

41

one of naked body parts, heavy breathing and sexual gymnastics over the photocopier.

I cheated a little, I admit, because confining the story almost entirely to dialogue was difficult, not to say a little boring. After all, two people finding themselves in this situation, even if they did fancy each other, would not necessarily break the convention of years and gabble away non-stop. There would be silences, even pauses of the pregnant variety. So I used flashback every now and then to conjure up memories, events and some emotions for the two characters to relive – taking them out of their situation in a different way, if you like.

And that is the main point about single settings: like an enforced holiday in a tiny caravan in a thunderstorm (yes, been there, got the damp T-shirt) they can be a little restrictive. So it's nice to get out and about for a change.

Making your characters move about is useful; not only for the storyline, but it can be a huge benefit for you, too. You are forced to think about maybe even small descriptive pieces to suggest moving, opening doors, seeing other people and so on. And all this can be interspersed with an ongoing dialogue which will make it seem more natural.

It also draws the reader into seeing these scenes with us, rather than concentrating too much on the characters all the time. A brief walk, for example, will encounter a varied background, which doesn't need to be painted in detail, but it will help give a change of pace and atmosphere. A character opening a door for another, buying a drink, helping with a coat – none of these events need to be huge in detail, because it's not necessary – but they allow writer and reader to make a more interesting journey.

I've found in the past that if I get a bit stale in a setting I'm writing about, moving the action to another room (the kitchen, readers, the kitchen!) actually makes me think more widely about my writing. Moving outside the building or even going on a car journey, will do even more. During a love story, for instance, moving from a small room full of quiet discussion, to a beach with crashing waves, provides a dramatic change of feel and a contrast in emotions and background.

But what if your story really doesn't call for a change of location, and you are restricted to the same scene? Well, you can do what I did and use flashback to see their story in another setting, with new descriptions and people. Or you can simply make them move in as realistic a way as possible.

Unless they're shackled to a bed, of course, people move all the time while talking. They stand up, gesticulate, look out of a window, hold their heads in their hands, pour a drink, light a fag, scratch themselves – all the normal mannerisms which you can intersperse with dialogue while allowing your characters to 'move'. Place them under emotional or physical pressure, too, and the movement increases by a huge amount as the tension mounts.

TOP TIPS

- Real life is constantly on the move – don't get stuck in a rut.

- Everyday movements give a more natural feel to the scene, as well as demonstrating or accompanying anger, passion, despair and so forth.

- A change of location allows you to bring a welcome change of pace and tone – and a freshness to what the reader is seeing.

- Describing movement in your characters can convey much about their age and physical characteristics.

Keeping It Going (continued)

Using the pressure-cooker

MY FRIEND DAVE ALWAYS claims to work best when he's under pressure. He's not a writer but a DIY enthusiast, and the pressure comes from his wife, Barbara. But even that saintly lady admits that when he has only a few hours left to do what he's been faithfully promising to do since last Michaelmas, he goes at it like a whirlwind and does a marvellous job. As she says afterwards, it's not always pretty to watch, but the result is spectacular ... unlike when he takes his own sweet time and ends up fiddling about until he trips over the paint tin or falls off the ladder.

Many professional writers also claim to do their best work when under pressure. In this case they're not simply talking about being under the cosh from their editors, who are bawling around their stogies about the presses being kept waiting. (If this sounds like anyone you know, it's purely coincidental). Some will be referring to the pressure of knowing they have a piece to do yet not having a clear idea of how the story or article will pan out – because they haven't written it. They will, of course, because they know they must.

While it's not a good idea to put yourself under this kind of pressure too often unless you can help it – or you're one of those strange beings who enjoys the stress – setting your own deadlines can occasionally be a useful device to kick-start those creative juices where sitting and thinking about it at length will not. It's what some might refer to as controlled panic. It is also a handy way of getting used to writing to a time limit, which could serve you well when taking on future commissions.

Writing for competitions (such as in those in *Writers' News* for instance) is one way of introducing yourself to working to deadlines. They always have a date by which your story has to be in or it will no longer be eligible. Not that I'm suggesting anyone should deliberately leave it to the last minute before making their submission just to motivate a great story; the organisers get plenty of late entries already. But the deadlines are always fairly generous, some of them several months ahead.

And this is the problem. For some serial prevaricators, anything which smacks of several weeks ahead may be *too* generous; with a date you can't see because it's on the next page of the calendar, there's a tendency to cogitate a bit or go for a series of long, writerly walks and talk to the trees, searching for that perfect plot, that un-rejectable idea. The inevitable outcome is that three months suddenly shrinks to two, then one, then two weeks, then … Suddenly, the deadline is gone and you've missed the boat.

If, however, you can get accustomed to shortening that deadline yourself, by working to get your entry off a month *before* the absolute last day, then you may find you can generate the determination to complete the job instead of staring blankly at the wall for weeks until you've cogitated yourself to a standstill.

As with my friend Dave and his paintbrush, when he knows he simply *has* to paint (or not eat – the choice is stark), a deadline can help develop a real focus – even a crispness – about your work which may be lacking at other times when you can take a more leisurely approach.

By way of another illustration, in a recent wildlife documentary a lioness was shown chasing a variety of game in a very half-hearted – and therefore unsuccessful – manner. The reason? She wasn't actually all that hungry, but simply going through the motions. (Well, she was a lioness, and when a springbok goes pronking by without a care in the world, what's a self-respecting big cat to do?) The missing ingredient was hunger – ie: urgency. The moment she began to feel hungry, she regained her role of lethal hunter.

We, too have a similar instinct when responding to urgency, and there's no reason why we can't apply it to our writing; in other words, we *can* do it because we *must*. There is no time to waste on choosing that elegantly descriptive word or that neat bit of dialogue, you simply go for it: open with a bang, then on to the next sentence, disregarding any waffle. Before you know where you are, you'll find you've done something that any manner of studied thinking would not have accomplished so quickly. Sharp, incisive, uncluttered. Finish off with some honest editing and the job is complete.

Of course, setting your own deadlines demands discipline and planning, along with the ability to brush aside distractions and get on with the job at hand. And there are ways of doing it which will fit into your everyday life. Before going on holiday is one good way; by the end of a holiday is another. Before the end of a quiet weekend and a return to the hectic day job can be useful, too, as can a day at home with nobody else around, if you can manage such a luxury. Anything, in fact, that you can use as a device will work, providing you stick to it.

As Dave's wife says, it may not be pretty to watch, but the results can be spectacular.

TOP TIPS

- Set yourself deadlines, even if not required by your target magazine or publisher.

- Bringing discipline to your writing sessions will help you make the most of the time available.

- Be realistic about what you can achieve – but keep trying harder.

- Imagine what each project might achieve to keep you focussed.

Keeping It Going (continued)

Follow that!

THERE'S A BELIEF COMMON among film buffs – perhaps amply reinforced by numerous dire examples over the years – that a sequel can never be as good as the original. Somehow, says the prevailing view, the follow-on to a successful hit always lacks a certain something which, in the original, caught the public imagination and had cinema-goers streaming through the doors in their thousands.

Personally, I'm not sure this is true in all cases. Yes, there have been some lamentable sequels which should probably never have seen the light of day. But I can think of some which have been an improvement on the first, for all sorts of reasons – the prime one of which is familiarity (of which more in a moment).

Take the *Die Hard* movies, for example, starring the king of dirty vests himself, Bruce Willis. Yes, they're over the top and outrageous. They're violent and ludicrously improbable, even – especially the vest which, given the 'celebriddy' excesses in Hollywood, probably has its own trailer and make-up team. But, I'll admit to enjoying them hugely, largely because I can suspend belief by its braces in a corner for ninety odd minutes and not take any of it seriously. And why? Not necessarily because they improve with each one, but, like the Bond films, they have the appealing hook of familiarity.

OK, so childish enthusiasms aside, what has all this to do with writing?

Well, if the rule of following a winning formula can apply to films, why not apply the same rule to your writing?

The fact is, nobody ever said you cannot write about the same characters more than once.

Let us assume that you are trying to come up with another

story, but finding the process a bit painful. Unfortunately, you cannot give up, because, as a writer, you need to keep the wheels turning before the machinery gets clogged up and grinds to a halt. The customary ways of doing this are to (a) borrow from life, (b) sit down and grit your teeth until an idea comes to you, or (c) simply get on with something entirely unconnected with writing and wait for that flash of inspiration which will come just when you are out of reach of your notebook. Or there is another way.

How about taking a look back over some of your short stories, and choosing your favourite? Sold or not, it doesn't matter. The idea is to pick one which *you* are happy with, and read it again. Go through it carefully until you are firmly into it once more, and can absorb the original feel of the characters, time and place. Next, consider something which does not normally occupy too much of our time at the end of a short story, whether as readers or writers: *where do they go to from here?*

Think about it for a moment. You have a story you are proud of. You have characters who are fully formed (albeit in your own head), and with whom you feel comfortable. You have a place and a time and – given that you didn't have everyone perish in a fireball at the end of your first story, which would be a bit of a downer – the potential for your story to continue beyond that final full stop.

In other words, you have the makings of a sequel.

Now I'm not saying you simply continue writing, picking up where your previous story left off as if nothing had happened and everyone will know what's going on. Plainly, that would be expecting too much and leave some glaring holes in the scene-setting, among others. But what you can do is take these familiar characters and their situation, and set about packaging them into another one, with different events and problems.

I have done this successfully more than once, 'borrowing' people, their personalities and circumstances, and simply moving them on to a whole new set of conflicts. In one case, a man and woman finished in one story by settling their many differences and going off into the sunset ... then emerged in another as a married couple facing danger and doubt. This new set of events, although based in the same setting, strained their relationship until they found safety and eventual happiness all over again. The fact that both stories were published in the same magazine made no difference, because the 'sequel' came out some two years later. In another, I simply made my characters older and gave them a fractious and monosyllabic teenage daughter (realism aplenty and conflict enough for several stories, in my opinion). I didn't change their personalities, nor the general tone of the story, which was humorous. But giving them a few more years and landing them with a totally new problem *did* produce a very different tale.

I suppose I could now leap forward a few more years and write a third story, this time about wrinkles, pension books … and an impatient, fractious and no longer quite so monosyllabic daughter, but that might be pushing things just a tad too far …

Still, look it this way; if Bruce and his vest can soldier on into further stories, surviving different kinds of murder, mayhem and dirt, then why can't your creations?

As a writer, you have to use whatever devices you can to produce the goods. Sequels may be the answer.

TOP TIPS

- Short stories need not be the end of your characters. They can be resurrected for other adventures.

- Check back over your previous work. Can any of it inspire new stories?

- Do previous characters have the mileage to feature in something new?

- Don't let previous ideas go to waste.

Kick-Starting Your Mojo

EVERYONE GETS STALE FROM time to time, or dispirited – especially when the rejections begin to land on the doormat like cluster bombs. That's when the blue meanies can set in and seriously dent your creativity and drive. There are various ways of combating this, from eating chocolate cake to chugging back mugs of cheap sherry or chewing your fingernails down to the bone.

But how about some less harmful methods?

These include getting out there and putting yourself in the frame of mind where you can be reminded about why you wanted to be a writer in the first place. Or simply barging through all the dark moods by sheer determination and bloody-mindedness, until you see the light on the other side.

Kick-Starting Your Mojo (continued)

Getting the buzz

I MET UP WITH a friend and writing colleague the other day, to discuss a forthcoming literary event we were doing together. For reasons of convenience, the fact that there was a decent coffee shop, and probably for the same reason salmon and wildebeest invariably end up treading familiar territory, we met at a local bookshop.

As if that were such a strain.

It was one of those barn-like places where books come at you from all directions, and, if you're of an easily intimidated frame of mind, you'll feel a little awed by the sheer volume of … well, volumes. But it could as easily have been one of the local independent bookshops, as the net result was the same: I felt a warm glow spreading through me like a virus – and it had nothing to do with the coffee.

And I have to admit that the visit did me a power of good. Because it took me right back to the years before I got published, when I'd find myself in a bookshop, eyeing up my favourite authors and wondering how they'd done it. How they'd got there.

And thinking: *I want to be part of this!*

By being part of, I meant being published – and there was, as there is now, such a huge variety of possible subjects to choose from, it was a little like being in a sweet shop and not knowing where to turn next.

That's not to say that this recent experience was instantly productive or impressive. I had the drive home to follow, during which many creative thoughts probably slid out of my brain and fell on to the hard shoulder to join the bits of shredded lorry tyres, the occasional shoe (why always one?) and the unfortunate wildlife which hadn't managed to join the chicken on the other side. But I did reach my PC with enough of a pleasant charge of energy remaining to make me sit down with a renewed sense of enthusiasm for what I was doing for a living.

And that was worth its weight in gold.

Writing being the solitary procedure it so often is, we can so easily fall into the habit of getting too wedded to our keyboard day-to-day, of simply having our minds cluttered with the very *idea* of being productive, come hell or high water. It's a bit like thrashing around in the sea and not going anywhere; it might look impressive for a while, but it soon gets tiring. This false productivity also comes at the expense of self-motivation, because it can leech away that fantastic yet hard-to-explain buzz which set us on the writing path in the first place.

A good way of resetting your writing default, therefore, is to re-acquaint yourself with the marketplace. And the only way of doing that is to get out there in it, even if just for an hour or so. Forget the internet and all those soulless sites which, although packed with colour, information and ease of access, simply lack the sheer atmosphere and tactile quality of a room full of books.

It means going to a bookshop or library and becoming absorbed by your surroundings. Pick up a book or ten and check out the blurb. See what's out there and allow yourself to take in the sheer volume and variation of published works, whether in your favourite genre or not. Check the latest publications and see what's hot – and who the publishers are. Do a quick word count to see what's current, and take a peak at how the opening couple of paragraphs are handled and compare them with your own style.

It's also worth looking at the strap lines on books. Yes, it's marketing-speak, and meant to catch the eye for a split second before the reader moves on. But do the snappy lines give you any ideas? Do they throw up an image in your mind? If so, what kind of strap could you think of for your current/future project?

Many books also contain a lot of information about the authors (their websites) and the publishers and agents (check the attributions pages). This is especially useful for the yet-to-be-published, and at least gives you a name to aim for when making that first submission approach.

Of course, some might say there's a down-side to being surrounded by so much published material. The very sight of so many books, many claiming to be 'best-sellers', can be a rather brutal reminder of just how much competition exists out there. Well, very true. But life is all about competition (sorry, kids) and trying to overcome it. Instead, take comfort from the fact that those authors on the shelves all had to start somewhere – and most of them probably did a lot of what you're doing right now before they got their big break.

The worst thing in the world would be to try and pretend that the successful authors don't exist.

The best thing in the world is to try your utmost to join them.

TOP TIPS

- What do you want to do – write or push words around?

- Renew your desire to get published by becoming absorbed in the marketplace.

- See what else is being published and compare it with your own writing.

- Take in the books on the shelves and reinforce your determination to put yours within distance of joining them.

Kick-Starting Your Mojo (continued)

Follow the leaders

IF YOU'RE TRYING TOO hard, the inspiration simply won't come, or your ideas seem dull and lifeless (or, as an agent I once knew would say cuttingly about my latest submission: 'Not this one, dear.') it might be time to take a short break from writing and see how others do it. Or, more accurately, take a look at others who do it and listen to what they say.

An easy trap for budding writers to fall into is thinking *I couldn't possibly do it like they can.* 'They' being the many authors who pop up at literary festivals and book fairs, to talk about their writing.

First, let me tell you, listening to established authors blathering on about how they overcame the slush pile and now spend their days gazing indolently across a lush meadow and rattling off the next couple of chapters before a leisurely lunch, has to be taken with a certain amount of salt. Rather, try a bucketful.

As everyone knows, getting to be a published writer is hard enough. Once you've got there, however, it's like any other job – you have to maintain the output to keep your place. And most authors don't do that by gazing at anything … other than maybe their sales ranking on Amazon or the progress of the postman with the morning's mail. Usually, they're too busy fretting about the progress of their next book and wondering how to explain to their agent that they need more time.

Sure, there are authors who give the impression of having it easy. And I won't be the only one to have had the teeth-grinding experience of listening to a less-than-modest author having an enormous smug about his or her writing day. I've often felt like letting rip with a bellow from the back row: 'OK, that's all very well for *you,* matey. But how can *I* get a bit of that action?'

Fortunately, those authors are few and far between, and it's been some time since I felt a squirm coming on at listening to some lofty scribe patronise an audience in this way. Instead, I tell myself that those who do are probably hiding all manner of insecurities I'd rather not know about.

Rather than kid ourselves that they must be hiding some wonderful secrets on how to get published from the rest of us poor souls, I believe it's better to listen between the lines and analyse what they are saying. Because therein often lies a simple, useful message.

Take the famous American thriller writer who described recently how he spends his time writing at one of several local Starbucks, because that way nobody can get to him without scouring every coffee shop in southern California. What he was actually saying was that he needs space – and *a* space – in which to write, away from distractions. Does that need for space ring any bells? You bet it does! We all need that, because, without it, doing what we do is so much harder.

Another writer described writing her books on a diet of chocolate. In reality, she wasn't bragging about being a binge eater of commercial proportions. She was describing a 'reward-for-effort' system of self-motivation to keep her nose to the grindstone. Basically, the message is that we all have to find our own method of pushing ourselves.

I heard one elderly writer, with TV credits going back many years, confide to a rapt audience that he still indulges in ear-wigging in post office queues to get ideas and keep up on current idiom. Although told in an amusing way, he was being absolutely serious – and how many writers out there rely on what they hear and see for ideas and background material? Given a guess, 100%?

The fact is, panellists rarely come across with truly awesome secrets to writing that best-seller. In fact, what they are usually describing, concealed perhaps by a witty or self-deprecating delivery, is more often than not a portrayal of a mundane day-to-day job. Because that's what writing is – it's a job like any other, a proving ground which has to be gone over afresh each time you sit down to write, whether it's your first story or your hundred-and-first.

Most published writers I know who have any degree of humility (luckily, most of them) share the same quiet thought: that they cannot quite believe their good fortune. They're not all making serious money, indeed most are doing other jobs to earn their keep. And, true enough, they wouldn't swap what they do for the world.

But they all know they have to keep producing the goods, whatever genre or writing field they work in. And that takes constant application and effort in writing, researching and editing. In short, the basics of what they do are no different than for the rest of us. The added pressure for them is knowing that if they don't keep at it, there's always someone else galloping along behind who will happily take their place, given half a chance.

Who knows – using the same application, that someone could be you …

TOP TIPS

- Look for events with established writers, and see what you can take away from what they say.

- Ask yourself: what are they doing that you aren't?

- Use their experience and success to give yourself inspiration.

- Remind yourself repeatedly: they had to start somewhere.

Mixing with other writers

THINKING RECENTLY ABOUT A writer's convention I had attended, I wondered what I had gained from it, other than a shocking headache and the ability to mumble incoherently after three late nights and too much coffee.

It's very easy to pursue our writing, whether part- or full-time, with one's nose to the grindstone and mind in gear, concentrating on the craft, without actually appreciating that there is more to it than that.

Rejections. We all get them, whether starting out or already established. And talking to other writers is the quickest way of discovering that rejection is simply part of the job – not something reserved exclusively for *you*. Talking at this conference to a well-established thriller writer, the conversation got around, as it invariably does, to 'the latest project'. I was surprised to hear that his latest book had been rejected. The fact that he had a successful series behind him had evidently cut no ice. Although disappointed, he was already working on another book, because the one thing you learn about this job is that you cannot wallow in misery – you have to pick yourself up and get going on something new.

It's the same, incidentally, whether writing fiction or features. Rejection is something you have to get used to; it is, as has been said before, only one person's opinion. (OK, when you rack up quite a few of those opinions it gets a bit annoying and depressing, but the argument still holds true).

Doubts. We all have 'em, like ticks on a horse blanket. Doubts about our ability, doubts about the market, doubts about whether we shouldn't go off and do something 'useful' instead. We have doubt in our make-up because it makes us stop and question what we're doing, a form of safety mechanism. But it should also make us try harder. Or different. Doubt you're writing the right thing? Strike out in another direction. Doubt anyone likes what you're writing? Get a second, third, fourth opinion. Doubt you'll ever be a published writer? Submitting your work is the best acid test you can get.

Talk to some authors, and you'll soon detect a measure of doubt in there somewhere. It might be buried deep, and it might be about all manner of things, from basic technique to giving a talk promoting the published book. But the writer who doesn't have some niggling worm of self-doubt inside is very unusual. Hang around with enough of them (and most writers are very gregarious people who love to talk about what they do), and you'll occasionally hear those niggles rising to the surface. But the good ones don't let them get in the way of their work. They simply push them down and get on with it.

Ideas. If there's one thing I do get from attending conferences, especially panels and interviews, it's ideas. I don't mean I sit there and nick someone's plot; I mean ideas about how to increase my work, improve my style or generally enhance my chances of getting work accepted. It can range from hearing an author enthuse over doing research (and focussing rather than getting bogged down by it), or through hearing a snippet of oft-repeated advice which I already knew about but have let slip for some reason. It could be hearing an agency name dropped, or that a particular genre of book is becoming popular, which I may have completely overlooked while stuck in my room for months on end, kidding myself I can write *and* keep an ear to the ground at the same time. (I can't, incidentally – which is why I need to go to conferences and author talks).

Motivation. Whether listening to unpublished, new or established authors, they can add to your self-motivation. Whether talking about their latest project, their writing style, their market research, agent, publisher or latest reviews, it's easy to detect a buzz in the air which can get even the most jaded of writers going again, determined to emulate them. I've come away from most events refreshed and itching to attack a particular aspect of my job, whether improving on an idea or simply doing something different or with greater enthusiasm.

Lack of motivation dulls many a creative thought, and one way of refreshing that motivation is to hear how other writers cope.

Progress. One question you hear quite often is, 'How's it progressing?' 'It' being the latest book, article or poem – or simply the writing generally. A few people might be somewhat automatic in this query, but most writers I know, especially in crime-writing circles, are genuinely interested and want to hear that all is going well.

The other 'progress' is more personal, and that's the progress you yourself are making, and how to ensure that you don't stall due to any or all of the points above. Progress in writing can only be achieved by getting down and doing it. But you also need to get away from the keyboard for a while, and mix with people of a like-minded nature. Working in isolation may be the ideal for most writers, and for many it's a difficult one to achieve. But there is such a thing as comfort in numbers, even if only for a while.

Even if the price you pay is a headache and the ability to mumble incoherently for a day or so.

TOP TIPS

- Take time out to visit writing conventions or literary festivals and mix with like-minded individuals.

- Absorb the attitudes and advice of other successful writers.

- Compare their advice to your own way of working and learn from it.

- Be determined to join their ranks.

Binge writing

FOR MANY PART-TIME WRITERS, it's not ideas that are in short supply. Nor is it plotlines or characters or the pure mechanics of writing. It's time.

The idea of having a few hours off devoted entirely to writing is something many people can only dream about. This may be a period found somewhere in the wasteland between work, family and all the other demands of modern living. It might be a few hours or minutes snatched from evenings and weekends, or possibly the occasional longer burst on holiday.

I tend to think of it as binge writing, when even a short bus journey was – and still is, incidentally – an opportunity to scribble down a few thoughts on paper, one hopes to be morphed into something coherent later.

It's surprising, though, to find how many people approach such valuable free time in blissful uncertainty, only to sit down and …stare at a blank sheet of paper, wondering what to do next.

Like all tasks, writing is something that requires as much planning as we can give it, and never more so than when time is a precious commodity. Dive in head first without a thought to planning the outcome, and it will soon slip away.

It's not unlike painting and decorating. As a boy, I used to think that all you needed was paint, a brush, something to cover the furniture and a radio blaring loud enough to make your teeth bleed. My father, a keen DIY-er, taught me otherwise (especially the radio bit).

He used to plan his decorating jobs like the crossing of the Rhine, with a full family briefing on colours, materials, tools and clothing, all checked and double-checked days before picking up a brush. This preparation for the preparation used to drive my poor mother up the wall, she being of the *Just paint the ****** thing!* school of thought. But she always understood this was necessary, because my father's time was in short supply.

Using his approach, planning a writing binge would run thus:

Windows of opportunity. Not a term my father would have used, but it helps to identify when you may be able to set aside time to write. That way, everyone around you knows what to expect.

Materials. With time of the essence, you need to hit the ground running, so to speak. This means having everything to hand, be it paper, pen, printer ink, notes and reference sources.

Task. Is it a new project or an ongoing one? If new, take time out beforehand to jot down a synopsis from which to work, so you don't slide straight into blank-brain mode or end up raiding the biscuit tin every two minutes because you can't think of anything to write. For an ongoing project, you'll probably have some ideas down already, aided perhaps by the last writing you did, and maybe some changes you want to make. Either way, you should be able to see a clear way ahead.

Objective. What do you hope to achieve during this writing stint? A page? Two pages? Solid (new) writing plus some editing? Be wary of aiming too high, and set a realistic goal *for the time available*. Lumping too much of a load on yourself will leave you stressed and dissatisfied – which might be reflected in your writing.

Dealing with distractions. Well, whoever guaranteed a smooth patch of utter bliss and quiet, with only the sound of a distant skylark to accompany your creative thoughts? If ever there was a day when your Auntie Minnie was going to call round for a cup of tea and a moan, you can bet your buttons it will coincide with you-know-when. If you can bear to do it, lock the door, unhook the phone, bury your mobile in the compost heap and tell anyone who might be in the habit of calling round that you've gone into rehab. Basically, lie in your teeth if you have to; you owe it to yourself.

Plan breaks. Actually, it's more a question of planning the amount of writing *in between* the breaks. Setting yourself a target that is manageable for *you*, followed by breaks away from the desk, gives you a series of work-plus-reward bursts which will help you focus on the best use of your time. The quickest way to lose concentration – and enjoyment – is to become stale and tired through sitting for too long without a stretch, a leisurely scratch and maybe a quick walk round the garden with a cup of tea and a biscuit to disperse the mental moths.

Review your progress. You can stand back and look at what you've done, probably best left toward the end of your writing stint; that way you can still make any quick changes you think necessary, note any extensive amendments you may wish to make next time and even revise the direction of your story in light of what you have just accomplished. Or you can leave any reading/editing until later, and make more leisurely decisions then.

TOP TIPS

- Plan when, where and for how long you intend to write.

- Have ready everything you need.

- Rough out a synopsis of what you intend to write.

- Don't tell anyone – otherwise they'll be unable to resist calling round.

- Take breaks – even if only for a few minutes each.

- Start planning the next binge.

Ideas and How to Get Them

'WHERE DO YOU GET all your ideas?' is one of the questions most frequently asked of authors everywhere. A fair question, you might say.

According to one well-known author, there is a little-known website called **www.storyideasRus.com**, where we all go when we need inspiration, and can download the next instant blockbuster.

There isn't, believe me. You think I haven't checked?

Ideas and How to Get Them (continued)

Learning to focus

A RECENT SHOPPING EXPEDITION to find a birthday present for my wife found me in a similar situation, writing-wise, to a friend who writes short fiction. Surrounded by a plethora of goodies, all suitable (and, what's more, all potential vote-winners in the pressie stakes) I dithered and shuffled like a nervous teenager on a blind date, not sure what to choose. Basically, (and here I hasten to say I depart from the teenager analogy – *my* teens, anyway) there were so many possibilities on offer I couldn't decide which one to go for. In the end, I allowed greed to heap disaster on me by snatching at something in haste … which, as it happened, proved unsuitable.

But back to my friend. He mentioned that in spite of an abundance of ideas, he had recently found himself in a cycle of constantly starting something, then running out of steam because he couldn't settle on where to go next. This had resulted in a string of projects, all abandoned at various stages and each resembling a lengthy art-house film: with no end in sight.

'Lucky beggar!' I hear you mutter. 'If only I had so many.'

The fact is, many writers experience moments like this, when they cannot settle on one particular task. So eager are they to get their ideas down on paper they flit from one to the other like a honeybee on steroids and end up making a pig's ear out of each one. I usually find it hits me just after I've completed a large or difficult project, as I slough off the mental concentration of the previous job and try to fix on something new. With ideas collected all around me, I find my wastebasket becomes full of paper balls, my PC games get a hammering and I tend to drift around the house like Marley's ghost.

This is where self-discipline comes in, and you have to rein back your enthusiasm for grasping at straws or launching into something without some forethought.

Begin by clearing your desk of all those project idea notes you've gathered, *save one*. Yes, of course the others are wonderful gems, harvested in the bath, on the train, or wherever it is your best ideas hit you. And yes, you want to write them *all*. But they are also a huge distraction. Stuff them in an envelope and put them somewhere temporarily out of reach, or give them to your neighbour with strict instructions not to let you near them for at least a week.

Now look at your choice of market. One way to help decide *what* to write, is to focus on the market you want to write *for*. Given that most magazines have a limited range of subjects or story styles they will accept, this immediately limits what you can work on. You should inevitably find yourself discarding all thoughts about writing anything that is not appropriate.

An alternative is to check the current stock of writing competitions. These may call for a genre or topic you wouldn't normally try, but as a discipline it will focus your thinking away from that vast plethora of ideas swirling around in your brain.

This is also useful in that as well as a subject goal, you are automatically set a time limit. There's nothing like knowing you have to meet a deadline for focussing the mind. It cuts out the temptation to dash off at a tangent – usually in pursuit of an idea which has just popped into your mind along with that little voice on your shoulder telling you it will be a real doddle to knock off in a couple of hours. It won't, of course, and you know it.

Another stumbling block to completing anything mid-stream is a lack of regular planning. This can be over a simple but important scene which, although small beans compared to the whole story, is enough to make you down tools in frustration and reach for something else.

Instead of letting this minor glitch derail your thoughts completely, take a long, hard look at the scene where you are stuck. On separate lines beneath it, type the key words of what you might want to happen next. (I generally use capitals to 'shout' at myself so I don't miss anything – even if I eventually discard a particular idea). Forget grammar and punctuation – simply put down the points you need to cover. For example, your key scene might have a character agonising over resigning from a high-powered but hated job, and the inevitable furore that will follow. You could end up with: FEAR – DECISION – DECLARATION – BOSS'S REACTION. Then think about what kind of scene could logically come next. You might end up with: FINANCES – OTHER CONSEQUENCES – ALTERNATIVES – WALKING OUT – FREEDOM – RELEASE. Repeat, as the old medicine bottles used to say, as needed.

In this way you are focussing on a small but crucial part of the story each time, instead of the whole feast. Rather than letting it defeat you, tempting you to grab hold of something else in the hope that it may be easier, you are building stepping stones towards completion of the larger picture. Before you know where you are, you've got the path forward to the next scene and can repeat the exercise as required, instead of pigging out on ideas and ruining all your hard work.

TOP TIPS

- Focus on one idea at a time. Trying too many at once will inevitably water down your efforts.

- Plan what you intend to do next and stick to it.

- Look for writing challenges (competitions, story websites requesting themed submissions) and see what inspiration they throw up.

- Read, watch and listen. There are ideas out there everywhere.

Catching Ideas

FROGS ARE, PRETTY MUCH, patient creatures. They can sit as still as a lump of mud, barely visible to the human eye, for what seems like hours. Maybe they have cracked the secret of life and don't need to do much more to get by. Or maybe they are simply bone idle. Whatever it is, they have the ability to wait for a hapless snack to come along, then lazily snap out their tongue and swallow a few easy calories without breaking sweat.

If only our story ideas came as easily.

Unfortunately, for most of us it doesn't work like this, although some critics like to believe that's all we have to do; simply sit in a quiet room and cogitate fiercely until our ears bleed.

The truth is that occasionally a thought pops into our brain out of nowhere and won't go away. Then, as luck will have it, when you desperately need a quiet space to grow the idea, you find everyone in creation is beating a path to your door. More often than not, however, you occasionally have to get out there and live a little.

Most story ideas come from things like activity, movement, sounds or colour ... all generated by the ebb and flow of things around us. And this comes from our connection to and observation of other people.

Some writers might claim to get inspiration from inanimate objects. Buildings, for example, or natural landmarks such as rivers, beaches or rolling hills and valleys. But without the eventual introduction of a human element, these things aren't all that exciting to write about because they have nothing to move them forward.

People-watching is a highly under-rated activity – even for non-writers. I know because I've done it all my life. Having spent many years travelling regularly around Europe, I can't think of a time when I found myself bored, even when waiting in some God-forsaken departure lounge for a flight in the wee small hours. Mostly I found myself absorbed by snippets of overheard conversation, or trying to decide what my fellow travellers did for a living. (Then, just as things were getting interesting, I usually ended up being dragged away by the call for my flight.) The same can happen in railway stations (waiting being part of the package), in motorway service areas, or even public libraries. Wherever it is, if you sit and watch people long enough, and if your curiosity isn't aroused even a little by the sight, activities or conversation of those around you, then you'd better check your pulse because you've probably stopped breathing.

When asked where they get their ideas from, many writers can't immediately say. This is because they can be inspired by snatches of events, often too fleeting and intangible to make a definite impact, or by a headline in a newspaper, as has happened to me. One second there's nothing, the next there's a fragment, maybe a passing thought, but sufficient to know it's there and can be turned into something concrete. After that comes the hard work of mentally chewing it over and watching it grow and blossom into a workable idea.

Of course, it's at this chewing over point that many a brilliant idea can hit the dirt, lost along with all those other astounding but ephemeral thoughts we have about holiday destinations, birthday presents and things we've been meaning to do to the kitchen tiles but have forgotten about several times already.

As you've been warned many times already within these pages, a notebook helps, or the back of an envelope. The margin of any newspaper or magazine will do, too, or even your own forearm if all else fails. As long as you write it down before it drops into the mental waste bin and is lost for good.

Whatever your method, you also have to be open to the signals, receptive to the idea that what you see and hear may appear to be bland and everyday, but could still have potential for a story. See a man in a smart suit taking a stroll by a riverside, for example, and try questioning the alternatives. Could he be meeting someone, or has he just had a bruising encounter and is thinking of hurling himself into the water? Are the two people in the background merely part of the scene, or could they be following him? Or – if you are a thriller writer – does someone now have him in the sights of a gun as payback for who knows what misdemeanour?

Ask yourself about the 'what ifs'. What if the man was running headlong, instead of strolling? What if the woman checking the train arrivals board at the station suddenly collapsed ... or saw a face in the crowd which evidently filled her with terror? What if the nice old lady walking out of the shop suddenly dropped her bag ... and a heap of stolen items rolled across the pavement?

In the hands – or head – of a writer, the mundane can suddenly take on an entirely different tone, and the chance snatch of conversation overheard in the queue at the post office (a prime location, in my experience, for some mind-boggling stuff) can start up a train of thought way beyond the original meaning.

The main factor here, is people. Without them, we might as well simply sit and wait. And catch flies.

TOP TIPS

- Watch people in everyday settings. Imagine what their story might become.

- Read headlines and think of alternative stories.

- Snatches of conversation can provide all manner of possibilities.

- Carry a notebook, record notes on your mobile. Even the briefest note can open into a big idea.

'Tis the season to be a writer

NO MATTER WHAT TIME of year you read this, Christmas will one day loom large on your radar, and you will be either relishing or dreading the forthcoming couple of weeks. Relishing it because you love all the festivities, are a mad party animal and want to get on *down*, or because you simply need a break from work; or dreading it because you don't *do* Christmas, possess the soul of a curmudgeon and want to punch Santa's lights out for being so relentlessly in your face.

Take heart, however; whatever your persuasion or nature, if you're a writer, this could be just the break you need to make it a productively Cool Yule.

Character studies. What better opportunity to build your latest characters than basing them on the steady stream of visiting rellies tramping through the house like a herd of wildebeest in search of water. You don't see them from one year's end to the next, you barely know their names or even where they fit into the family tree; so why not hijack bad-tempered Uncle Bill as the model for your current villain, or gossipy Aunty Janet as the meddling old busybody who comes to a sticky end in chapter four? Nobody will know, will they? Hardly any of them read, anyway.

A word of warning, however. Most families have a Rumour Network Co-ordinator (usually one person), who has the name and contact number of every living relative – and even a few who have passed on beyond life's final chapter. And this is where your supposedly secretive character-stealing will be revealed, and you could face a familial row that would make an episode of *Eastenders* sound like *Stars on Sunday*.

Atmosphere. Every Christmas gathering has it in spades. There's joy, of course, and love, and often a sprinkling of things in the air like redemption, forgiveness and tolerance. OK, they might not last longer than the first pulled cracker, but if you're quick, you'll be able to catalogue them.

Tension. Usually of the sort you could cut with a piece of soggy lettuce. It tends to rear its head when gifts turn out to have come from the local garage forecourt late last night. This ignition point is usually signalled by a senior female member of the household rising wordlessly to her feet and going into the kitchen, leaving a chill in the air like the second Ice Age … followed by the ominous clunk of the pedal bin. Or there's the gloriously un-PC joke rattled off by Uncle Bert, completely unaware that the vicar is out in the hallway and he's a staunch believer in hot pokers in uncomfortable places.

Conflict. Similar to above, but often sizzling just beneath the surface. And if you think conflict only includes drawn swords and pistols at dawn, wait for family feuds that have been simmering for decades to break out over the cooking sherry.

Stories. There's no story like a true story, and families can provide fertile ground to the writer in search of an idea. You don't have to mirror Granddad's account of his part in Rommel's downfall, or Aunt Lil's memories of the Blitz. But, if you listen, you'll find that there are things some family members have seen or done that can act as a springboard to your writing far better than staring into space or eating your own bodyweight in Hobnobs. And if your current storyline needs the background to tracking the disintegration of what seemed like a wonderful family gathering, all you need do is watch and wait …

Thinking time. When else do you have an excuse to go for a quiet walk with no other aim than to let your brain go into free-fall? There's no office calling you, no project awaiting your boss's approval, no pub or coffee date with your mates to draw you away or occupy your mind. So, while everyone else is lying around like beached haddock, you can take advantage of their inability to move by sliding out of the house and going for that walk you've been promising yourself. Don't forget to take a notepad with you, because you may just get a belter of an idea, and it would be criminal to let it go to waste.

Writing time. Now this, of course, is the Promised Land for writers everywhere. But it might not be possible for everyone because of family commitments. However, if you are one of those for whom Christmas is a glorious and welcomed opportunity for doing absolutely nothing, with no interruptions and all the time in the world, why not kick back and settle down with a glass of something pleasant, to catch up on that writing you've been too busy to do for so long? Turn off the phone, put the television into storage, arm yourself with whatever you require to write … and simply write.

A final word of warning, though.

Alcohol is a great liberator – and I should know, because I've written some of my best work with a large glass of wine at my elbow. However, as I've also discovered, it can liberate the creative brain to a point where what seems witty, insightful and brilliant on the screen is actually, in the cold light of day (usually the following day) a load of old tosh.

So, moderation in all things. Enjoy the break and whatever this season means to you, but, whatever you do, keep writing.

TOP TIPS

- Use the break to do some rough drafting.

- Study people for character traits you can use in your writing.

- Watch faces and actions for instant mood portrayals.

- Take some time alone to walk. And think.

Ideas and How to Get Them (continued)

Tell it like it is

MY OLD GRANDMOTHER HAD a saying which went along the lines of: *Now there's a face you could chop wood on.* That this was obviously not very complimentary hardly needs saying, and implied the person in question should be shunned by polite society and hustled out of town on a one-way bus.

But what it really did – especially for an impressionable youngster like me – was build a powerful mental picture of a face ... usually one to be avoided.

And this brings to mind a problem facing many writers: of putting a face to their characters without going to extremes. And this is nowhere more challenging than in short fiction, where every word is vital and not to be squandered on endless description, yet where you need to communicate at least a sense of what your characters look like.

Some writers use the 'famous person' trick, such as 'his face bore a hint of Harrison Ford' or 'she had the willowy look of a young Grace Kelly'. While this instantly gives the reader a visual anchor, you have to be careful; peppering your story with an array of look-alike Hollywood stars or the cast list from your favourite soap can be a hindrance, especially for readers who have no idea who this or that character might be. For many readers, suggesting A looks like character Z from a soap doesn't actually describe them at all if they have never watched the programme.

But how do you conjure up a face which you can describe adequately, or which has some feature (such as blue eyes) which you may need to refer back to later in your story without suddenly turning the eyes brown instead? Sometimes, getting the right detail to the reader can be a problem.

By its very nature, the more remarkable the face, the easier it is to describe, simply by virtue of a specific characteristic or 'hook'. But how do you describe a face which may seem right for your character, without going to the extreme of giving him a feature which makes him *too* noticeable? In this case, you need to use the more mundane, yet obvious, such as eye colour, bone structure, shape or skin features, yet without losing that image as your story moves on. And the simplest way is to use real faces.

However, I'm not suggesting you go round leaping out on complete strangers and taking their photographs. This could lead to a closer acquaintance than you might like. Instead, you could use magazines and clip out those faces which strike you as interesting or remarkable. They may have a firm jaw, for example, or deep laughter lines, a weak chin, petite nose, a mole on the cheek, eye-catching beauty … anything which draws your attention as being appropriate for one of your current – or future – characters. This way, instead of trying to describe a suitable face from your imagination, you have the picture in front of you, available whenever you want it. Furthermore, the detail in magazine pictures is clear and easy to study, whereas with time, a mental image can fade and disappear altogether.

The same trick can be applied to scenery. It is difficult to conjure up, say, a scene in a public park without referring to the commonplace – pathways, lawns, bandstand, flower beds or children's play area. But that scene could be anywhere … and nowhere. Far better to go out with a camera and take some shots of your local park, so you have some solid order to the features described above. Ten to one you will also pick up some minor, yet important added details such as clumps of grass, wind-blown litter, a tangled chain on the swing or a faded kite caught in a tree. This will end up sounding more authentic, yet can be described in far fewer of your valuable words than you might otherwise use. For other scenery in the locality, why not resort to brochures from your local tourist office, where the photos are usually of excellent quality and often helpfully descriptive of the architecture and history?

Mood can be another awkward writing hurdle. Your story

might call for the description of a building possessing an air of menace, for example. Dark, yes. Forbidding, even. Gloomy, certainly – all words you could use to good purpose. But if you can find a genuine building with all those attributes, you will undoubtedly notice other important features such as windows like eye sockets, sagging gutters, pitted stonework, crumbling cornices – in fact a host of brief, descriptive labels which will do a nice job of bringing out the atmosphere you need.

Oddly enough, in a country where discussing the weather is a form of etiquette, describing it can be surprisingly difficult. Try writing authentically in mid-July about snow, or at three in the afternoon about a foggy night. We all know the feel of light rain, or the stickiness of hot sun or the pleasant chill of a morning mist. But getting out there in any of these conditions and making notes about how they interact with other features such as trees, hills, traffic, buildings and so forth, will add enormously to the authenticity of your writing without giving you an attack of migraine. And it will be far easier to put into words which suit the context of your story.

TOP TIPS

- Strong physical characteristics stand out. Look for them in others.

- Use photographs of people and faces for inspiration.

- Capture weather and light to help describe atmosphere and mood.

- Use real structures or buildings to help give reality to scenery in your stories.

It's the little touches that count

ANYONE SHORT OF BACKGROUND material for a story? That little touch to add colour to your scenes? I picked up plenty recently, all in one cycle ride in London.

As a member of a cycle marshal team in a night-time charity walk around the city, along a route of 26 miles and with 15,000 (mostly lady) walkers to encourage, help and watch over, my writing hat had been parked on its hook for the night in favour of a crash-hat and a supply of chocolates (well ... nobody said we *all* had to suffer ...). I was therefore thinking of things other than storylines, plot points, deadlines, editing and how to get biscuit crumbs out of the keyboard – a sort of alternative writer's retreat, if you will.

Part of my duties was to keep a roving eye on traffic conditions, single walkers, limping walkers, walkers going off-*piste*, leery drunks, clubbers falling out of doorways and finding themselves face to face with a phalanx of ladies in decorated bras – more scary than you might think, even sober – and generally not doing a prat-fall off my bike in front of everyone.

In this fairly relaxed state of mind, I couldn't help but notice some unusual, albeit unforgettable sights. There was the stern lady walking resolute but alone, whose face lit up when an elderly gentleman stepped out of a doorway as she approached and smilingly doffed his cap. There was a pair of young tourists, luggage in hand, who stared in wonder as the walkers trooped along the Embankment and past the London Eye at two in the morning. There were two mallards in St James's Park, standing quietly side-by-side as the human tide went by, totally fixated and somehow part of the event. A policeman in Horse Guards Parade, gun held across his chest, alert and aloof, yet nodding occasionally in approval. A young WPC on traffic duty, looking on wistfully as the column crossed the road under her direction.

And a young man (very drunk) at 3 a.m., who asked me what the *@!* was going on. When I explained, he became suddenly sombre, before waving off his friends and staying to add cheerful encouragement to the walkers. (We didn't understand all the words, but we certainly knew the tune).

I watched an urban fox near Vauxhall Bridge taking advantage of sandwiches left in bins, and some cheeky pigeons, ignoring the official mayoral line about not feeding the birds, picking up their share, too. The edifice of the MI6 building, sprouting cameras and spiked fences, loomed sinister and forbidding in the dark, yet, improbably, within touching distance of every walker who passed by.

Buses filled with night travellers were the target of walkers, the passengers encouraged to wave back and show their support, and even emergency vehicle crews speeding by seemed aware of events while concentrating on other things.

There were many more such sights which came and went during the night, some poignant and human, others inanimate and fixed, all there to be looked at and stored in the mind or forgotten at will.

And suddenly I was in writer's mode again, spotting scenes where others might not, noticing faces looming out of the dark, some smiling, others creased with effort, but each no doubt with their own tale to tell.

Amid all these images and sounds was a welter of material, ideal colour for any genre, from human relationship dramas through to crime thrillers. All the elements were there for me to use, colourful and sharp; all I had to do was pick them up and let my imagination do the rest.

It would be nice to think I could build something solid from any one of the sights I have described above – and maybe I will. But what I recall most vividly were flashes, mere glimpses of things seen and heard which have stayed with me. Instead of using them as major story lines, I will probably employ them in more subtle ways as background colour to future stories: the dark, chilly recesses by the river; how my skin felt stretched and cold; the taste of tiredness in the mouth; the wind rustling discarded paper; ambulance lights bouncing shadows across shop fronts; the throb of an unseen helicopter high in the sky; a shop alarm in the distance; a figure in the bushes of Battersea Park; a pale face in the gloom by a darkened building; a siren from a riverboat, haunting and atmospheric; and a mournful howl from an inmate of Battersea Dogs' Home, no doubt sensing that, while he was locked up inside, we lucky humans were outside having all kinds of fun.

That's the city sights and sounds taken care of; next I need to take a ride in the country, to remind myself of what that has to offer, too.

TOP TIPS

- For your individual scenes and backdrop material, think how small touches can add colour to your story.

- Wind, light, shadows, the hiss of tyres on wet roads, voices arguing, the scuff of shoes on concrete – use them to add atmosphere.

- Sounds carry in a different way at night from how they do in daytime. Night-time in a city is no longer as quiet or deserted as it once was. Your storyline can therefore be set at two in the morning just as easily as two in the afternoon.

Ideas and How to Get Them (continued)

Trawling the past

STUCK FOR A PLOTLINE? Not sure about how to kick off a story? Need to add that extra dimension to your idea to make it different?

Well, you could do worse than to go back in time.

I don't mean you should throw in your lot with the contemporary and start writing historical themes – unless, of course, it's your chosen genre, especially with the resurgence of interest in historical settings. Neither do I mean the over-use of flashbacks in your stories. These are useful, but too many of them can become laborious.

The method by which many writers have found exciting ways of using the past is as a springboard for a story set in the modern day. This might begin as an event in history but, skilfully blending fact and fiction, links into the present day so that it affects a cast of modern characters. No need to name them, but certain books centred around the Knights Templar have achieved spectacular success in this manner, spawning a whole new industry of literature, films and video games. While some criticise the 'facts' in these stories, and even more the writing style, nobody can argue that they haven't been successful, or that readers haven't enjoyed them – surely the whole point of writing as entertainment. I would also hazard a guess that writing and researching them was great fun for the authors, too.

A similar use of times gone is the 'past misdeeds' plot, where someone with a fuzzy history suddenly finds that his indiscretions aren't as well buried as he thought. Cue threatening letters or emails and the 'Send me some dosh or I'll tell all' scenario. Another is the 'remembered hurts' angle, where Character A has not been the nicest person in the world, and it looks like he or his family members are about to get sliced and diced by a mysterious Character B hell-bent on revenge. The areas of tension centre on which, of the countless people they were nasty to, is coming after them, and what did they do to earn such hatred in the first place? (Naturally, both parties have to be intrinsically horrible, mainly because coming back to slap someone with a bunch of daffodils simply because they wouldn't give you a decent Annual Performance Review, while very understandable, doesn't really rate as an exciting read).

An additional element is: will the secret avenger get away with it – and do we as readers want them to? A third person here is useful to investigate and solve the puzzle, because, at heart, while nobody likes Character A for being such a cad, we don't feel much sympathy for the bitter and twisted Character B, either.

A variation on this theme is to have an otherwise innocent central (but naturally spunky and resourceful) character placed in danger due to a past event of which he or she has no direct knowledge. This could be through a family link, a case of mistaken identity, being in the wrong place at the wrong time or because he's plain damned unlucky.

If you are looking for a plot idea involving a link with the past, try trawling through the history books for an event which could echo forward to the present day. The last fifty years is littered with enough wars, financial crashes, commercial failures, murders, assaults, political chicanery, and others, to come up with a whole host of viable scenarios.

Whichever way you play it, the tension is in (a) the character finding out about the threat/danger in time and (b) unravelling the puzzle to avoid ending up as dog meat.

There are a few points to bear in mind, however.

The linking of periods can be an effective way of adding colour to a story, but remember that you have two sets – maybe more – of cultures, periods and characters, all behaving in accordance with their times.

Make sure your timeline is accurate. If you have people from the recent past, they have to be of an age where, if they are a threat, they are a credible one. Nobody would give much credence to an aged wrinkly with a dicky ticker and a Zimmer frame (unless he had a heavy with a bolt through his neck to do his bidding). Similarly, be prepared to show your characters coming to grips with different time-frames. It rings true if a dark avenger coming from the middle ages has trouble coping with modern living, rather than if he or she adapts in a flash. Personally, I always find it odd when someone from the distant past doesn't instantly wet their pants on seeing the pace of life today, or one from the future appears to have no problem using a telephone directory to track down the target!

Remember that the real world is no longer quite the same as it once was. Cities were smaller, communities closer, borders sometimes non-existent and travel times different. (Well, I did say different – not better!)

Historical accuracy should also be observed carefully. Playing with unrecorded details is fine, if of an inconsequential nature. But if you cite a major event or figure in history as part of the background, getting it right will add to the story. Getting it wrong will not.

TOP TIPS

- Check your historical facts.

- Make sure your timelines are believable.

- If relevant, note differences in language, dress and manner.

- The threat has to be credible.

Ideas and How to Get Them (continued)

See what floats to the surface

ONE OF THE MORE common questions asked by writers starting out in this business is, 'I've got a problem: with so many ideas whirling around in my head, how do I settle on the right one to write about?'

Call that a problem? There are writers out there who'd give their granny's right arm to be so discombobulated! I'm rarely if ever short of an idea or several, but there have been times when the only one I've had has been so lonely and miserable, I've had to take it out and shoot it, to put it out of my misery.

The nature of ideas is that they come and go like last week's news, rarely hanging about unless you write them down as soon as they occur. (Note to self: practise what you preach; last week I couldn't be bothered to stir myself and reach out for my notebook in the middle of the night, and an idea went walkabout. All I know is, it was a belter. If it should float your way – grab it.)

The human brain has a great capacity to be attracted to certain things over others. Laughter over misery, comfort over cold, chip fat over limp lettuce … But the subconscious works in ways we can't explain – or, at least, *I* can't. And one thing I've found over the years of slaving over a hot keyboard is that there's a degree of natural selection at work in our heads. It makes sense, therefore, to rely on that inner skill when deciding which direction or choice to take.

What you might need to do is give that internal selector a bit of a nudge every now and then, otherwise you're expecting too much of it. The first thing is to organise your ideas in a way that makes them instantly 'grabbable'.

Picture if you will, the mind of your average writer (and for this, I use my own as a model, so don't feel I'm talking about *you*). It's pretty much like a wheelie-bin (or a compost heap, according to my wife) full of all kinds of rubbish, none of it recycled and most of it swirling around and fermenting nicely. To make sense of this pile of festering flapdoodle, you need to sort through it and arrange the good bits into recognisable 'tags', so that you can pick them out at a glance.

This is where the idea of the 'elevator pitch' from the film industry comes in handy, where a writer has the length of time it takes to walk to the elevator to pitch an idea to a producer. It helps if it can be contained in a single line.

Thus, if one of your ideas involves a small boy being abandoned in the jungle, where he is brought up by wolves and befriended by a singing, feckless ape and preyed upon by a nasty but clearly well-educated tiger, you could describe it as:

Small boy, jungle-reared, journeys from man-cub to man-child. Would make a fantastic feature-film!

OK, I cheated with that last bit (and there's not a writer alive who doesn't fantasise about getting a film deal). But you get the idea.

Speaking personally, trying to recognise my own ideas in any other way is far too confusing without using this brief kind of tag. But it's enough to remind me what the idea is about without needing to look at all the detail or the notes I might have made about sub-plots, characters, locations and so on. Just like the elevator pitch, it relies on a sketch, rather than the full picture. And writing these single-liners down (on separate pieces of paper if you like, to distance them further from each other) allows me to sort through them to see what appeals.

However, don't rush it. What I do is allow the selection process to work by leaving the ideas to one side for a few days, then going back and running my eye down the list. Doing this, I inevitably find that one will suddenly look less attractive than it once did, compared to the others. So I lose it; dump it back whence it came, maybe saving it for another time.

This is where the brain uses the interaction between the eye and the subconscious, drawing you towards what appeals most, and away from the ideas that feel less worthy.

Repeat, as they say in cookery books, until done, or until

you find that the same idea keeps floating steadily to the surface, or your eye keeps being pulled back to one more than the others.

It's at this point that your writing really begins, because, by this time, the creative part of your subconscious will also have been chugging away quietly, giving your initial idea more strands and directions to work on and expand it into a tangible storyline.

TOP TIPS

- Turn each of your scribbled ideas into a single, brief sentence with just sufficient detail to make them recognisable.

- Look at this list over several days. Prune away any which do not instantly appeal.

- By reducing the list, you are forced to concentrate on a narrower range without wading through too many distractions.

- DON'T throw away the discarded ideas – you'll come back to them someday.

Ideas and How to Get Them (continued)

Writing about people

IF NON-FICTION IS more your bag, or you simply want to try dipping your toes into the article-writing market, the human interest angle seems unlikely to go away anytime soon. It seems we love reading about other people and delving into their lives, whether out of genuine admiration or, as a cynic might say, because they appear to have a more interesting/ shallow/dangerous/glamorous time than the rest of us.

Sadly, though, if we take the front covers of many magazines as a guide, this insatiable nosiness appears to centre on clueless celebs, falling out of nightclubs three sheets to the perpendicular.

However, before dashing off to the nearest club with camera and notebook in search of an exclusive, it's worth noting that the field of 'celebriddy' interviews, while high-paying for the right subject, is already very competitive, even over-fed. And most of the writers currently working that arena have a contacts network to rival MI6, and will have taken a long time and constant feeding to acquire it.

There are, fortunately, plenty of other human-interest areas to consider where you can develop your skills, many of which are about people with whom readers can identify. Examples are: ordinary people in extraordinary circumstances; people with unusual hobbies or backgrounds; unsung local heroes doing special work; or simply people who make a difference to their community and those around them. These are all potential subjects for a write-up.

Before starting out, it pays to plan your target market. Quite simply, the kind of magazine you write *for* will generally have a bearing on the type of subject you write *about*. Will it be the women's magazines market, which has a voracious appetite for human interest stories? Or maybe newspapers, local or national? Or will you aim at more specialist and trade publications – maybe one with a subject you have some detailed knowledge of? Whichever you choose, as always, study the market to see what kind of articles they run and how they are presented. Do they include photos (most do), and what is the average word count? Do they go for straight text or do they include side-bars and bullet-points to break up the presentation on the page? Are they inclined towards a serious tone or do they take a more light-hearted approach? All of these points are necessary to bear in mind when approaching an editor with a proposal. Anything too wildly off-target will fall at the first fence. Once you have these firmly sorted out, you can plan how to come up with the goods.

Lists. Assuming you have a subject in mind, decide what you want to cover in your chosen article. What, for example, do you feel is noteworthy about this person and the world he or she inhabits? Then compose a list of the questions you need to ask to draw out the meat for the article.

Angle. Editors are always looking for a fresh approach or a new angle – especially on a previously covered story. Is there anything special about this person which nobody has thought of before, which will lift it out of the ordinary and get it noticed?

Technique. Thrusting a digital recorder under someone's nose in the hopes that he'll blather on constructively is not recommended. Unless you plan it with care, you could end up with a vast amount of material, much of it composed of gaps, pauses, whistles, barking dogs, passing traffic and head-scratching. It might also be your subject's very first interview, in which case he will be nervous. Ask if he minds you recording his words. If you haven't prepared your strategy first, you could end up with a lot of navel-gazing but not much else.

Photos. Generally considered a must these days. A decent digital camera is relatively inexpensive and easy to use, and good quality photos help to illustrate the article and make it more saleable to an editor. As for the subject, it's a rare individual who wouldn't be pleased to see themselves featured in a magazine article, and if it helps get you the information you need, so much the better.

Check your facts. If unsure about something the subject may have told you, don't be afraid to say, *Can I just confirm that you said ...?* This often results in him or her adding something else you can use.

Time. Don't just turn up hoping for an interview; make an appointment. And don't out-stay your welcome, as your subject might be a busy person with one eye on the clock. If you can, set the parameters for the length of the interview beforehand. Be business-like, professional and aware that it's their world you have stepped in to.

Dress for the occasion. Going to an office? Dressing accordingly is a professional courtesy. A farm? Think animals. Mud. Machinery. Effluent (especially effluent). Factories can be noisy and cold. Turning up in glitzy shoes and a T-shirt might make you look cool, but it won't help your concentration to be uncomfortable, or to have various animal by-products oozing through your best Jimmy Choos. (Yes, sexist, I know, but the imagery is so much better than Russell & Bromley or Clarks).

Don't delay. Write the article while it's fresh in your mind. Illegible notes, a duff recording or perceived memory are dangerous things for a writer. Also, think about whether you could use the same material but with a different slant for another magazine.

Then get on with the next one. As in all things, practice makes perfect.

TOP TIPS

- Look for gaps in the market.

- Decide on an angle to use which nobody else may have thought of.

- Photos will help sell the article.

- Check and re-check all the facts. Then check them again.

Ideas and How to Get Them (continued)

Write it as you see it

IT IS OFTEN CLAIMED that everyone has a book in them. I'm not sure if it's true, as I know a few people who admit they wouldn't know where to begin, even if they were offered free champagne and a fortnight's cruise in the Caribbean.

This rather contrived link brings me to another dubious belief among would-be writers: that anyone who takes a holiday to somewhere foreign could write a decent travel feature.

True, there's nothing like writing from personal experience or knowledge. That's why professional travel writers spend a great deal of their time out of the chair and in the air. Just because a holiday brochure says a resort is quiet, genteel, secluded and exclusive, doesn't mean there isn't about to be a vast, noisy, disco-themed nudist colony built right next door.

To write convincingly, it helps to live it. And like a couple of instances recently, where best-selling non-fiction books turned out to be entirely fabricated, with a subject like travel, if you don't do a proper job, you will be found out.

Remember also that the travel-writing scene is very crowded, which means you are going up against serious competition. It makes sense, therefore – especially when learning the craft – to look for a market where there might be a few gaps.

One of the markets which is always on the lookout for well-written pieces, is on the family activity front. Sadly, this is unlikely to mean jetting off to the Maldives and wallowing in the sun, sea and sand for a few days, before knocking off a quick piece about what a great place it is but pity about the lack of things to do. (I heard someone complaining about this recently – having knowingly booked two weeks on an exotic 200-ft wide sand blip in the middle of the Indian Ocean. What did he expect – a branch of Disney World?)

Writing about activities closer to home is both kinder on the pocket for the beginner, and easier to find, research and visit than anywhere overseas. There's also a ready readership potential, because, with ever-tighter budgets, families are always looking for somewhere interesting to visit during weekends and holidays. And with the number of magazines aimed at this general market, the possibilities of success are greater if you can produce the goods.

Look for something different. Repeating an item already covered extensively is unlikely to arouse an editor's interest. They want something with an unusual angle; something new, exciting or which hasn't been covered for a long time. I once wrote a piece about Bletchley Park, home to the Enigma code-breakers in WW2. However, my piece wasn't about the technical wizardry involved – that had been covered already. What I discovered was that a WREN stationed there during the war is now a tour guide. I was, in effect, covering old ground (a place to visit – not the WREN) but with a very human angle, making it of greater interest to the editor and readers.

See it yourself. There's nothing like getting hands-on experience, as the actress said to the bishop. If you discover something specific about a visitor attraction which might not be mentioned in the usual guide books, then that is a worthwhile hook to dangle in front of an editor. And the fact that you have seen and enjoyed it yourself will come through in your writing.

Get all the facts. You are, in effect, recommending somewhere to others. You should provide all the information they will need, such as location, opening times, restrictions, admission price, facilities and so forth. Saying that it's 'roughly ten miles from X, and should be open in April and probably won't cost more than a couple of quid' will not endear you to an editor – and nor should it.

A picture saves words. Travel or activity pieces, whether of sand blips in the Indian Ocean or an amazing hike in the Cairngorms, come alive with some decent photos. They catch the eye when a page is turned, and may make the difference between (a) your submissions being accepted or not, or (b) your feature being noticed by the chance reader.

Give it the bullet. Bullet points, bold headers or side bars are nuggets of information which can be absorbed quickly. Editors like them because they break up the page.

Timing. It helps if you submit your piece in good time, say, prior to school holidays. Writing in September about an attraction that is closed all winter is not helpful. Equally, any natural aspect of your piece (say, the presence of bats for a specific period, or the beautiful sunsets) should also be considered, as they will impact on your submission being taken seriously.

Vox pop. Comments from the staff, manager or others about what is on offer helps give a natural feel to the piece, and makes it less like an essay.

So, with that in mind, plan accordingly and ... may your holidays be fruitful!

TOP TIPS

- Start with a local attraction to get a feel for what you need to do.

- Include photos to back up your text.

- Look for an unusual angle – something which will hook the editor.

- Read other examples to see what information they include.

- Give the piece some legs: angle it to suit various magazines and their readers.

Get out of the garret

HEARD ABOUT THE LONELY writer who struggled in his garret for fifty years, bent over his trusty Adler (a sort of early virus-free word-processor) ignoring all other worldly distractions in order to produce the perfect story? By the time he emerged triumphant, fingers numbed, back aching, blinking into the daylight and clutching his hefty manuscript … the world had gone digital.

To the other extreme, take the ever-gregarious wildebeest. Some experts believe they don't group together simply because they happen to be going in the same direction, or for security against marauding carnivores. It's more mundane than that; they band together because (a) they like to chit-chat and exchange news, views and grass recipes with other wildebeest, and (b) because nobody else understands a wildebeest quite like another wildebeest.

As writers, it goes without saying that we need a bit of piece and quiet to get the ideas out of the bone on to the paper. We can't all produce best-sellers at a corner table in a café or on the 08.15 to Paddington. But it's worth remembering that there is a world out there – a world containing a lot of other writers, all sharing the same hopes, burdens and fears. And it's surprisingly easy to lose sight of this and become too isolated for our own good, fixated on the idea that the only way to write effectively is to shut ourselves away.

This was brought home to me recently while talking to a new writer. She was amazed when I happened to mention that I experience the occasional rejection letter. This seemed inconceivable to her, based on a firm belief that, as a published writer, everything I now write – even on spec – must be automatically accepted, a sort of Gold Card access to the coffers of the publishing world.

How I wish!

Some might call her naïve, but further discussion revealed that she had never talked to other writers, published or otherwise, and had therefore built up presumptions which had never been corrected.

The fact is that we all need to network with others of our kind, in order to share common experiences. And this is probably more important for writers than many others, because we engage in what is arguably a fairly lonely way of passing the day. Some might dispute this and say they are able to work quite happily on their lonesome without interaction. Fine. But toiling away in a garret was never meant to be an industry standard!

There are ways, of course, for new writers to 'plug in' to what is going on, and pick up on some useful secrets and tips along the way. Joining a writers' group is one, and there are plenty dotted around the country, usually meeting once a month. This may not be everybody's cup of tea at first, faced with a group of confident faces with tales of output, word count, competition successes and how they are just waiting to hear the good news about their latest submission. But don't be put off; most groups are welcoming and eager for fresh blood (in the nicest possible sense), and will usually encourage members to show/read their work for analysis by the rest of the forum. While criticism in such a face-to-face manner can seem a little daunting, the wise writer will cherry-pick the comments and gain some gold dust to take away with them. The benefit is that being able to talk about your writing is a surprisingly useful way of making you think about it in the wider sense (as is being able to comment on the writing of others). As a consequence, you might well spot ways of adjusting and improving the way you work and develop some ideas for future projects.

Literary fairs or exhibitions are also great meeting places for writers of all genres. The subjects under discussion will inevitably be broad, and you might have to pick and choose to find your particular area of interest. But these events often include workshops hosted by professionals, where writers of every level can pick up all manner of information and advice about the art of writing, as well as how to go about the basics of doing background research, making submissions and finding a market for their work.

Book signings and talks (usually held in bookshops) are also ideal trawling places for picking up tips and ideas. Most published writers are happy to share their experiences, and since most of them have come up through the ranks writing short fiction or features, you could say there is some degree of common ground.

On a more personal basis, finding a like-minded 'buddy' to talk to is invaluable. Especially on a cold, wet Monday, when the postman has just dumped another impersonal rejection through the letterbox. One way to counter this swift kick to the vitals is to take time out and talk about it to another writer over a cup of coffee, because ten to one he or she has experienced it, too. And remember, one of the best ways to combat a rejected story is to promptly send it off somewhere else!

In short, problems which may have seemed insurmountable can often be brought into a clearer perspective when aired with someone who understands what you do ... and most of all, why you do it.

Garret-hound or wildebeest ... or a mix of the two? It's your choice.

TOP TIPS

- Too much isolation can kill off creativity.

- Ideas need the compost of outside contact.

- Mixing with other writers can stimulate ideas and ambition.

- Talking with like-minded individuals is refreshment for the soul.

Ideas and How to Get Them (continued)

Giving your characters their head

I USED TO THINK, back in my early writing days, that when it came to portraying action and dialogue in a story, the approach had to be as rigorously controlled, say, as when describing scenery. And that these two more malleable elements of fiction writing had to be kept in check like unruly children, something fundamental to being a good writer.

Unfortunately, as I soon discovered, controlling what happens on the page – especially in longer projects – needs a high degree of planning and forethought. Because, without both, you can soon find yourself wandering off-track like a drunk after a Saturday night shindig. The consequences are that your hero or heroine might follow suit and do or say something you hadn't planned, thereby ruining your whole idea.

OK, call me weak, but being a fairly fly-by-the-seat-of-my-chuddies type of person, I gradually began to find that, every now and then, I would relax my guard. Before I knew it, one of my characters had flown off at a tangent and begun to act in what a builder friend of mine refers to as 'off-plan'. This meant I found myself typing dialogue or action which seemed to be controlled less by me than by the story unfolding on my screen, and that events were occurring in a way which bore no relation to my original plans.

Don't get me wrong; I don't mean I began communicating with the ghost of Raymond Chandler, or that Elvis started dropping by in the wee small hours to show me he'd been a frustrated novelist all along. (I might get a little intense when deadlines loom near, but every one of the voices in my head is my own – I promise.)

The nearest I can come to describing this is like skiing off-piste, which I've only ever done by accident. It's interesting, if a little unsettling, because, like writing, if you veer off-course instead of following the flagged routes, you can never be certain where you'll end up.

At first, strict discipline (or a carefully prepared plot layout) will probably ensure that you haul your errant ideas back on course, bringing them into line once more. This usually avoids considerable re-writing and the frustration of feeling you've just wasted a lot of time and word-power.

But if you think about it, while a structured approach can be beneficial, especially if you have a deadline to meet, it doesn't have to apply every time. Why not let your writing become organic once in a while, allowing the direction of the words or action to be dictated by the subconscious?

I don't mean chuck all your planning out of the window and abandon yourself to undisciplined scribbling – that would be a little too free-form, especially if you hope to earn money from your writing efforts. But if you try it when you are not too pressed for time, you might find that when you read over some of your unintended diversions, you discover that they aren't necessarily bad, and have actually flowed effortlessly on to the page instead of having to be dug out with a pitchfork.

One explanation for this organic growth in the story may be down to the characters becoming fleshed out in your mind, and developing naturally into the sort of people you meant them to be, rather than simply following a clinical plan.

Nowadays, perhaps because I have learned not to be too straight-jacketed in my approach, while I generally have a vague idea of the direction I want to go in, I find I have a far looser hand on the controls when it comes to writing action and dialogue.

This came out most strongly in a recent story, when my lead character, faced with the situation of rescuing a particularly evil individual from death, simply walked away and left him to it. Nasty ending, perhaps, but take my word for it, it couldn't have happened to a nicer person.

I hadn't planned this; in fact, my original idea had been to have the villain done away with in a twist-in-the-tail scene by one of his equally vile colleagues. Yet when faced with the scene on the page, I found myself thinking that, given the kind of person the hero was, and what he knew of the villain, would he really risk life and limb to save him – or worse – chance him escaping the law and continuing his wicked deeds elsewhere?

The wonderful thing is, within the bounds of reason, you can have your heroes and villains do whatever you choose. They are your characters, after all, inhabiting your scenes and therefore subject to whatever you choose to throw at them. This means they don't have to act, speak or emote in a conventional manner. And if you think they should behave a little off-the-wall, well, why not?

A bit God-like? Maybe. I prefer to think of it as part of the creative toolbox, where you elect to use a variety of means to achieve the finished product. It may not work every time, and occasionally the tried and tested methods may prove more practical. But every now and then, why not cut loose and give your characters their head? Let them speak or act in a way you hadn't planned, to see where it takes you.

Live dangerously (on paper, anyway). You never know, it could prove liberating in all sorts of ways.

TOP TIPS

- Be prepared to let characters dictate the action and see where it leads.

- Don't be too inflexible in how they speak, act or react.

- Review your cast of characters and see if any of them could take a more central role.

- If you find yourself automatically allowing a character his head, go with it.

- They're your characters – do with them what you like.

Ideas and How to Get Them (continued)

Writing humour

THERE'S A VIEW AMONG some aspiring writers that the only thing you have to do to write humorous material is to string together a list of jokes. That this doesn't work will become painfully obvious by the speed with which rejections hit your doormat. The fact is that many editors – especially magazine editors – say they receive very few useable examples of humour, which surely leaves a space to be filled by those who can do it successfully.

First, what's the difference between comedy and humour? My rule of thumb is that comedy is performed – often, but not always, before a live audience – and intended to raise a laugh. Humour aims more at achieving a wry smile or at the most a quiet chuckle. (Unlike an American business colleague of mine who once spent an entire flight from Paris to Toulouse, hooting like a Thames barge when I unwisely showed him a copy of a humorous book I was reading. Apart from the embarrassment of being sat next to this gurgling idiot, I hadn't got the heart to tear it off him, so had to make do with the in-flight magazine instead, which was no fun at all).

Ironically, writing humour can be a serious subject; what strikes one person as amusing may hit the next like shingles. But some magazines are prepared to consider lighter material if it fits their subject matter.

This is perhaps the key guideline for budding humour writers: produce something geared to the wry appreciation of a subject close to a reader's heart, and you may strike lucky. In a magazine about caravans, for example, an item most likely to get a caravan enthusiast smiling is a humorous piece about caravans ... or anything associated with them. It's a question of making a connection. Describing a journey from A to B, for example, could be mundane and, on our current busy roads, about as funny as gangrene. The same journey with a line of washing caught on the back, however, might take on an entirely different tone.

The first thing to do is – surprise, surprise – study the market. In this case, identify those titles containing light or humorous material. Then zero in on those where the subject matter appeals to you, or is 'open' in nature.

Ask yourself whether the tone and content indicates that readers do not take themselves or the subject matter too seriously. Does the editorial show a tendency to swipe fondly at anything surrounding its core subject? Are the other articles light-hearted? Are there any cartoons? If the answer to these points is yes, then plainly a degree of humour is acceptable.

The next point is to identify a gap. Most editors like to vary the content, and much of it these days is of the 'quick-bite' size, digestible between other tasks. By its nature, humour material falls into this category.

Once you have a feel for the magazine's slant, then you can start building something around the subject matter which will appeal to the editor (most important), and thus the readers. And if you can treat the subject humorously, yet with a degree of knowledge, rather than simply ranting on about your favourite *bête noire*, there's no reason why you shouldn't succeed in getting a foot in the door.

The idea of trying to get inside the mind of a magazine reader might seem a little daunting, but, in the main, readers who regularly buy a particular title do so because they have specific interests. The advantage for us is that this makes their likes and dislikes easier to identify.

Pitching unsolicited humour to an editor is like any other kind of writing; there's a lot of competition. It's a numbers game, so the best way of approaching a magazine is to suggest multiple-choice ideas. Give them an A, B and C to choose from, and you might stand a better chance of getting beyond an initial weary glance on a cold, wet Monday morning.

Assuming you have three ideas in mind, make them as varied as possible. If the magazine has recently done a piece (funny or not) on, say, the spending habits of young women, they are unlikely to repeat it too quickly. Spread the net as wide as possible, and your submissions have a better chance of attracting a second look.

Whatever the topics, they should fit the tone and style of your target market. Whether you use a first-person 'opinion' piece (seen through the eyes of the author), or an anecdotal 'interview' style, there should at least be a solid basis to the article and it should reach a conclusion (humorous, preferably) rather than droning on like 'Disgusted of Tonbridge'. If your article, as well as being funny, has something readers can learn from, so much the better. Just because it's humour doesn't mean it can't be educational.

Most importantly, the article should not offend readers. You are writing to entertain, not cause apoplexy over their cornflakes. It can even – subject to the editor – inspire discussion, which is why some letters pages feature loud support and vitriolic condemnation of the same subject in equal measure – and many of them are a riot.

TOP TIPS

- Don't offend the reader just to be funny.

- Avoid starting open warfare – controversy has its limits.

- Go for a chuckle, not a belly-laugh.

- As a benchmark, think about what makes *you* smile.

Writer's Block ... or Not?

THERE ARE AS MANY theories on the phenomenon known as writer's block as there are on UFOs and monsters in Loch Ness.

I prefer to believe in the last two.

An inability to write *what* one wants *when* one wants can be due to stagnant thought, tiredness or simply trying too hard. But it doesn't mean it's permanent.

Try going for a good, brisk walk and letting some air blow through the attic. If that doesn't appeal, try writing something completely different.

104

Forcing the issue

I WAS ASKED NOT long ago if there was any way (short of sticking pins in my eyeballs) of forcing a scene or a storyline to come out from where it was lurking in the dimmer recesses of my brain.

The question was put by a lady who said she had numerous scenes in mind for a book she was working on, but simply couldn't seem to get going on them. Every time she sat down to write, she found herself stuck for how – or even where – to begin, and was wondering if she was suffering from writer's block.

The answer was: no. Intimidation by a blank sheet of paper, maybe. Fear of going off on the wrong track, highly likely. Trying to cope with too much detail at once, almost certainly.

But how to overcome it?

I have only one way, which I use regularly, whether for entire storylines or individual scenes. It consists of what is known in email and texting circles as 'shouting' – in other words, typing in capitals.

I used to receive emails some years ago from a work colleague who did this, and if ever there was a sure-fire way of getting the red mist to come down before I'd had my morning coffee, it was seeing an email from him. 'HI, ADRN.' he would bellow. 'HOW R U TDAY? NEED TO C U 4 A MEETING.'

Quite apart from his near-incomprehensible messages, it reminded me of my grandfather, who was stone deaf and thought everyone else was too. Being spoken to by him was like sticking my head out of the window of a fast-moving car. With my colleague, I tried shouting back, but he didn't even notice. In the end, I barred his emails and pretended he didn't exist.

There was an upside to this annoying episode, however,

because I now use something similar to help thrash out scenes in their initial stages, allowing me to move past the vague 'this guy walks into a pub' concept. I take a scene I have in mind, but shy away deliberately from writing it in detail. All I want to do is get the basic idea down on paper. (That, usually, is all I do have – the basic idea – and if I try writing it in full from cold, I'm likely to find myself bogged down on a particular point which might eventually have no relevance to the story.)

Let's imagine I have a central character entering a pub to meet a contact. I may be unsure about where it's going beyond this, but, if the idea won't go away, it seems attractive enough for it to take up space in the story, and I want to get it right. Where do I start? Quite simply, I splurge.

PUB – GLOOMY – FEW CUSTOMERS – LOW TALK – MIRRORS – SMELL FOOD/BEER – FAMILIAR PERFUME? – STICKY CARPET – COLD ATMOSPHERE – WARY GLANCES – SINGLE WOMAN IN CORNER – ORANGE JUICE – BRIEFCASE – CHECK OUT REAR EXIT – APPROACH – OFFER DRINK – SIT.

OK, that's really little more than a collection of random words. But those are what initially occur to me as visual points I might want to cover in the narrative. Some I'll use, others I may discard as being irrelevant or unnecessarily specific. The ones I keep are like stepping stones in my story, and once I set out to link them up, it won't be long before I have a comprehensive scene taking shape.

The next scene could be my central character's flight from the pub; he or his contact has been followed and he decides to run (Well, I didn't say he was a *noble* central character, did I?)

COLD DRAUGHT – TALK STOPS – CUSTOMERS LOOK UP –- WOMAN PALES – SHADOWS IN DOORWAY – SHOCK – DRY MOUTH – HOW FOUND? – RUN – DIVERSION – BACK DOOR – SHOUTING – CAR PARK – AWAY.

Of course, some scenes write themselves without this free-form block-lettering approach, but others don't. This is how I tackle them. I can worry about the specifics later. Given enough scenes or ideas treated this way, it means I always have something I can turn to rather than sitting like a rabbit in the headlights waiting for inspiration to smack me between the eyes.

And this method isn't solely useful for individual scenes. It can be employed on a grander scale in short stories, novels, chapters – even non-fiction pieces. With the latter, it becomes a list of points to mention, but the idea is still the same: to give yourself something to start with. The idea is to let the mind's eye float across the high points, and join up the dots afterwards.

Naturally, there are plenty of other ways to skin a cat (apologies to the lardy one currently blocking my view of the screen). But the strange thing is that I've tried *not* 'shouting' at myself, I really have. And it doesn't have the same impact (which is probably exactly what my mother used to say years ago).

But, if big letters work for mc, and it helps me get the words out of the bone on to the paper, who am I to argue?

TOP TIPS

- Block-letter the initial idea first – no matter how rough.

- Don't get bogged down in detail.

- Visualise your scene's main points – the stepping stones.

- Be prepared to discard some words or associated ideas.

- Delete the block-lettering as you go, as a sign of progress.

Writing from cold

THERE ARE TIMES WHEN even the most disciplined of writers, head bursting with ideas and plotlines, eager to get on with their current project, will sit down in front of a keyboard ... and promptly grind to a halt. For whatever reason, although pumped full of positive thoughts and intentions, they don't know how or where to start.

It's not so much the dreaded writer's block which afflicts them, but something more common, yet thankfully, much easier to deal with. It's a kind of inertia.

It might be compared with going to the gym intent on having a good physical workout. But finding yourself faced with all that complex equipment, such as treadmills, pulleys, weights and pedals, you freeze. Sometimes the brain simply cannot tell the body where to go first, and you end up in a half-hearted session with no real benefit or outcome other than a feeling of frustration and tiredness.

The only answer is to start somewhere simple, with a gentle exercise.

Writing from cold is another kind of warm-up, only with the emphasis on using the brain instead of the bodily muscles. And in the same way that a session stretching on the mat or walking on a treadmill for a few minutes can ease one's way into a routine, using a warm-up exercise on the keyboard can perform the same function.

The easiest way to approach this is to take a look out of your nearest window, and make a mental note of what you can see (not what you *know* is out there – different thing altogether). The scene doesn't matter, nor does the time of day or night. Nor should you try to capture every detail. What you are looking for is a current snapshot, including maybe one or two items which catch your eye the moment you see them.

Now go away and write that scene in one sentence – two at the very most. Whether you write in storytelling mode or straightforward descriptive style is up to you; the important thing is to write what you see and make it as interesting as possible.

Next, ignoring anyone real who might be out there, add to that scene by bringing on a person. What gender or age he (or she) is, what he is doing and why, whether he arrives or is already in place, is entirely up to you and your imagination. He might be walking a dog, kicking a brick or simply standing looking at the scenery. He could even be up to no good, if you feel that works.

Now bring in something to which your first character has to respond. It could be the arrival of another character. It might be a vehicle or even the ringing of a mobile phone.

The important thing is, something must happen to bring this possibly mundane scene alive. You could add to it by supplying dialogue between the characters. Perhaps a greeting to begin with, a familiarity between them which speaks of past knowledge, or a question which pinpoints them as strangers. Are they friends, colleagues, competitors or enemies? Have they come to this place on the same errand or are they on opposing sides?

What you are setting up in this exercise, in addition to getting your physical writing muscles working, is a small story or a scene in which there is action or conflict. More importantly, you are easing your brain into writing mode, that strange mix of imagination and creative moulding where you begin to think less about hitting the keyboard (or worse, cleaning it) and more about organising a scene and its associated characters, first in your head, then on to the screen. In other words, you're doing what you set out to do, just like every day when you are writing normally.

In the same way that athletes go through a warm-up routine before focussing on a specific training programme, writers sometimes need to flex their literary and creative muscles first before they get started on their current – or next – project. And rather than trying to jump straight into a scene and come up against a brick wall – the equivalent of muscle cramp for an athlete who hasn't prepared well – approaching it in a more relaxed manner can pay dividends and save a lot of frustration and heartache in the end.

Now, this scene might go nowhere. It could fizzle out before you've got a grain of a workable idea from it. But, subconsciously, you've been quietly getting yourself into the 'zone' – that area and mood you need to be in to get your creative juices bubbling over effectively.

Moreover, there's the possibility that you've been creating something new, something useful, which you can save and put on the back-burner, ready for the next time you are searching for an idea.

And the one thing you can never have too many of is ideas.

TOP TIPS

- Describe a setting – any setting – then add to it to build a potential story scene.

- Let the brain run free; don't focus hard on any one thing.

- Add more people or actions – anything which makes you keep writing.

- The physical and mental activity is merely getting you into the habit for what lies ahead.

- When you feel ready, save what you've written and get on with your current project. The scene you have saved might serve you well in the future.

Problem Solving

THERE'S USUALLY A WAY around every problem encountered in your writing. What it takes is time, effort and sometimes a bit of lateral thinking. Just occasionally it takes lots of coffee and maybe an understanding shoulder to cry on.

Mostly the solution is staring you in the face.

Problem Solving (continued)

What if …?

MANY NOVELISTS – MOST NOTABLY thriller writers – and screenwriters set out with a grand premise and scope to their work. This is usually based on a 'what if?' question with far-reaching effects, usually involving great peril and lots of screaming. Examples are as varied as 'what if there was an earthquake in xyz city?' to 'what if a cruise liner turned over, trapping all the passengers inside?'.

But you don't have to be a thriller supremo or screen wizard to apply the same 'what if?' technique to your writing. It can be used on a far smaller scale, but still have a dramatic effect on your storytelling.

A story's journey usually takes the reader from A to Z, with a few diversions along the way, hopefully wrapping with a satisfactory ending all round. But, all too often, merely relating the story this way is not enough. Even writers need a few surprises, something to occasionally jolt us out of ourselves before we can think of surprising the reader. This is at its most evident when describing a scene or a series of events, but we find the narrative unfolding in a dull, lacklustre way. It's as if the delivery is on a conveyor belt, plodding and steady but without giving rise to question what might be coming next. Basically, it lacks any real surprises.

A way round this is to ask ourselves a 'what if?' question. But rather than setting it as an epic premise for the entire plot, such as having a ship turn turtle in the channel, or a seismic shock hitting New Malden High Street (not that I have anything against New Malden) we should try applying it to a particular scene or even a specific character. Sort of epic, but on a more localised basis.

What if your central characters are in a car on a lover's tryst, and they have an accident? What if character A enters a house in search of a vital clue, only to find somebody else already there? What if the hero's gun jams? What if the vital key doesn't fit or the passport turns out to be a forgery? What if a damning letter or birth certificate has been left lying around? What if …?

A good 'what if?' can be used to drive events to unfold in a way readers will not have expected. It alters their expectations and takes them off at an angle, catching them by surprise.

In real life, a plausible 'what if?' might be the wife or girlfriend of a bank robber being unable to resist using a couple of the stolen banknotes at the supermarket, or popping some of the swag into a savings account (as happened not long ago) thereby undoing the robber's otherwise faultless crime. Or a philanderer (now there's a word you don't see very often) forgets something at a hotel, and they send it to his home address, providing damning evidence of his extra-curricular activities. It could be that the character you (and your potential readers) have taken to be one of the good guys, is actually not. Or that someone with what appears to be a clear and believable identity is not who he says he is.

'What ifs?' sometimes occur without prompting. Most writers like to think of them as Flashes of Brilliance – that part of the creative process which, to outsiders, means we often seem to be staring into space with the pained expression of an egg-bound budgie. But they're there nonetheless. It's as if the brain is moving ahead of its own volition, creating events without our having consciously thought about them.

However, you don't have to wait for this process to happen. Raymond Chandler famously suggested that when a story gets boring, bring in a man with a gun. Result: instant action and reaction, and endless scope for the rest of the story which you might not have considered originally. If you're surprised, think how the reader will react. Of course, it doesn't have to be a man with a gun; it could just as easily be a woman with a sledgehammer, sporting a breezy smile and a set of blood-stained dentures. But it's still an example of a 'what if?'

It's like standing at a crossroads and deciding where to go

next. Straight ahead is perhaps too predictable, even to you. Or do you turn left or right? Look at your characters, check the setting and circumstances that have brought them there, and ask yourself 'what if ...?'

Of course, the answer has to suit the context of your story. You couldn't reasonably introduce a shipping disaster if your story was about relationships in a small rural community. I mean, yes, it might work ... if you were in Hollywood with a few gazillion to blow on a wildly unlikely premise. Otherwise, you have to be a little more grounded in your thinking.

TOP TIPS

- Ask yourself if your story needs a change of direction.

- Does the proposed 'What if?' fit the context of your story?

- Is it believable?

- Can you write it into the plot without adversely affecting the rest of the narrative?

- Do you need to prepare the way in your back-story, or can you simply drop in your mini-thunderbolt and let events unfold as they will?

Writing out of sequence

THERE WILL BE TIMES when, as a writer, you have all the ideas you could wish for, you know where your story is going and you know what you want to say ... yet you suddenly find you've got stuck and can't go forward. It may be something very simple, such as the completion of an idea, a question of dialogue or narrative.

I liken it to seeing your way across a very muddy field; you can make out the gate on the other side, but there's no clear path for you to follow.

Sooner or later this happens to everyone, whatever their experience. But don't panic. Some people can, literally, write their way out of it, ploughing forward through sheer doggedness. Others aren't so lucky and have to sit and think their way clear of the jam. But there is another way, although to the new writer it might at first seem illogical.

You will often read of experienced writers quoting something like: 'Tell the story. Don't worry about the detail.' This follows the belief that trying to put in all the colour and detail of a story as you go simply slows you down, and it is better to go back later to flesh things out and complete whatever editing may be necessary.

Well, it sounds simple enough, and there's a lot of practical sense to it. It's what we do as writers, isn't it? We tell the story. And like any story, we start at the beginning and plod on until we reach the end. QED, as my old maths master used to say. Quite easily done.

But let us assume you have reached a point in your writing where you have a clear idea of the general plot; you may have sketched out in your mind the next couple of chapters or scenes, but suddenly you're struggling to put down the next move.

Every time you begin to write, you dry up, suddenly lost for the next piece of action or dialogue.

Well, this is where the 'Tell the story' bit comes in. And, like crossing a muddy field, you either work your way round an obstacle or you jump over it.

Let's go for the second option, if only because working our way round a large muddy patch takes too long. Jumping over is far more direct.

But where's the logic to this, you might say? Surely we'll lose the thread. How can we keep the sense of the piece unless we take each step in order, as it happens? Isn't that how we're supposed to write?

Well, not really. Nobody ever said you *have* to write in strict chronological or sequential order. Yes, it's nice if you can, but not always feasible.

By jumping ahead, what you are doing is diverting your mind away from a sticking point (the muddy patch) and concentrating on something where your thinking (the ground on the other side) may be a lot clearer.

Let us assume for a second that you have a scene where your central character (X) has discovered a body. The plan you are working to dictates that X, being a resourceful lone hero, will expose the killer sooner or later through the careful uncovering of clues. But, for reasons of dramatic tension, you don't want that to happen yet. Does X go to the police with his discovery (thereby being a wimp and shortening the story)? Does he study the scene and uncover the clues? Does he run? Call a friend? Ask the audience? Have a cup of tea and a sticky bun? What?

Rather than staring helplessly across your muddy field, why not jump ahead and worry about it later? This is writing – you're allowed to do what you want, as long as it gets the job done.

Think ahead. You may, for example, have a scene in mind where X is interviewed by the police, having been accused of the murder. This will be a powerful scene, full of tension and verbal interplay. You are relishing creating the strong characters to match the situation, with the possible outcome for X looking bleak until you spring the way out.

So why not write this scene instead? This is part of the 'Tell the story' advice. You'd planned on the police interview, anyway, so instead of fretting over a part of the plot you can't quite visualise, concentrate on a more vivid – but just as important – piece instead. Be careful, of course, not to introduce changes of timing, location or detail which may impact on the earlier passage.

Once you step back from a writing problem, it's surprising how often you find that it ceases to be one. Then you can go back with a fresh mindset to the scene you had been struggling with before.

You may find that this method of writing-in-reverse will spring other ideas and plot-lines. If it brings an added twist or surprise to your writing, think what it will do for the reader.

This approach can also be used in non-fiction. Get stuck with one paragraph of an article and you simply move to another. You were planning on writing it, anyway, so take the easy way out. Once accomplished, all you have to do is review what you have written and continue the part you had left earlier.

TOP TIPS

- Treat each obstacle as a challenge to overcome.

- Gloss over a sticky patch – you can always come back to it later.

- Write about something you *can* see, rather than struggling with something you cannot.

- Concentrate on writing something – anything – and new ideas will emerge.

- Think about what will come next.

Problem Solving (continued)

As simple as BCA

A COMMON QUESTION FROM writers is: 'How do I get my initial, basic, writing-a-note-on-the-back-of-my-best-friend's-neck idea to grow into something I can call a story?'

Well, there are probably lots of ways. And I should know, because I've tried most of them. There's the starting at A and going through to Z method; or starting with the ending and working backwards; or even cannibalising two or more unused stories into one. To paraphrase the old cliché, desperation can truly be the granddaddy of all invention.

Many methods of creating a story from a smidgen of an idea are pushed by the subconscious. We don't actually think about the workings of the process involved; it just happens, be it over days, weeks or even years. For the lucky ones, there won't be any effort – the idea will blossom into something fully fledged, the words tumbling out of the brain and on to the paper, thus avoiding all the wailing and gnashing of teeth that most writers go through at some time in their lives. (And for those of you who never wail or gnash … you lucky, lucky b …).

I recently set an example for a 50-word story competition, with the basic idea being that a woman working in a bookshop sees her love-rival arrive. She goes through all the emotions of such a situation as she watches the other person, until finally she throws a serious wobbly and drops a very heavy book on her rival's head. Result: accidental death and end of love rival.

OK, so I was aiming at dark humour here rather than high drama. But if we take the premise and run with it, what do we have? It's a story of love, hate, jealousy, rivalry, resentment and finally, uncontrollable fury. A bit like Prime Minister's Question Time, really, isn't it?

But how do we make this idea grow into a full story? Where

do we start?

Well, let's dispose of convention for a moment. *You don't have to start at the beginning.*

I have touched before on the dreaded writer's block, and advised circumnavigating a 'muddy' patch – a scene where you were 'blocked' for some reason – and jumping ahead to write a future scene. This is a useful way of freeing up your mind by concentrating on something else, until you can come back and write the sticky scene later. Another way is to break the proposed story down into 'chunks' or scenes, and deal with them as separate units. Then all you have to do is bring them together like links in a chain.

Some writers (me included) occasionally begin with a scene that may be somewhere in the story, but rarely at the start. Usually, it's because we have a vivid picture of what we want to write, and it pretty much tells itself. We then go back later and compose what might be the introduction.

If we take our bookshop avenger (BA), the scene which called to me the most was the final busting of the bubble where she climbs a ladder and a huge book manages to 'fall' on her love rival's (LR) head. (OK, so how many really huge, potentially fatal books do you find in bookshops these days that wouldn't be banned by a health and safety nut? But this is fiction – work with me here).

Writing this scene might be your first choice, too. On the other hand, the story needs some background. Who is the lucky person who has two lovers vying for equal air-time? It might be a man, or – let's be liberal – a woman. How old are they? How did they meet? How did the BA find out she was being cheated on? Or is LR the one being supplanted – the cheatee – if you wish? That's for you to decide.

The scene where BA watches LR walking round the store has a lot of potential for word-play in BA's mind as LR browses the various sections: Mind & Body, Psychology, Fantasy, Medicine, Horror … and especially, CRIME.

Equally, you could tackle BA's motivation as she lurks behind the shelves, plotting her rival's downfall. What will be the outcome in her own mind? Might it change her relationship with her lover – or does she give a hoot? You could, stepping out of the bookshop for a moment for a change in pace, try a scene where the person at the focus of these two women's attention is preparing to meet one of them. This could act as a way of setting up a scene where our sympathies may undoubtedly go away from this far from innocent party to one of the characters he/she is cheating on. But which one?

Wherever you start in your story, your writing is the most important thing. Each scene has to be consistent in quality, and must eventually fit seamlessly with other scenes. You have to bring them all together to form that whole story, from beginning, through the background, to building up the tension right through to the final, dramatic ending.

TOP TIPS

- Don't try to write the whole story at once – break it into separate pieces or scenes.

- Tackle whichever scene appeals to you at the time.

- Gradually flesh out the backgrounds of your characters, building description and narrative as it occurs to you.

- Constantly ask yourself whether what you are writing helps tell the story or not.

Bring on a stand-by

SOME NEW NEIGHBOURS MOVED in recently down the street. Nothing extraordinary about that; people move in and out all the time. However, for what should have been something of a non-event, excitement-wise, there has been a fair bit of activity on the village grapevine ever since they showed up and kicked the agent's board into the long grass.

Quite apart from the usual gossip at the shop, where information is traded like pork futures, along with eggs, papers and Mrs Green's farmyard honey, there has been much chat about what these newcomers are up to. Speculation is rife about 'shrouded' deliveries (bricks and cement powder wrapped in clingfilm to prevent damp) and the arrival of 'certain equipment' (grinders, tile cutters and saw benches, mostly). Oh, and let's not forget the blue Portaloo in the front garden, which has raised more than a few eyebrows.

Depending on who you listen to, this perfectly innocent looking family of 2 + 2 and a dog, are (a) converting the house into a doomsday survivalist bunker, or (b) creating a marijuana factory complete with giant fans and drying kilns, and anyone walking past it to the post box each day will get as high as a kite on the fumes.

Actually, all they have done, God bless 'em, is to make our lives a little more interesting by bringing a whole new dynamic to what is normally a quiet – some say unchanging – community.

And if you are in a similar position with your current writing project, I would heartily recommend you try introducing a new, walk-on character or two, to spice things up.

I mentioned before the 'bring on a man with a gun' device, when you need to give the reader a jolt. This advice – attributed to Raymond Chandler – is merely a way of introducing a burst of tension and/or danger and violence. (Well, it would, wouldn't it?)

However, not everyone writes stories where a man with a gun would be realistic. But most writers get to a stodgy bit occasionally, where things get a little … uninspired, shall we say. I know I do.

Introducing a new (unarmed) character is less dramatic, but it can be a useful way of changing the pace in a subtle way, and even leading to you bringing a different tone to the people he or she meets up with.

Let us assume you have a scene with your main character at home, preparing to go out to an important meeting. (It doesn't matter what the scene is, I'm merely plucking an example out of the ideas box.) Your problem is, you aren't sure where to go next. You may well have an idea leading up to the meeting, but you might feel that it doesn't link up in a coherent fashion, or is too big a jump in the storyline.

A way round this is to parachute in an entirely new character, purely at random, and see what happens.

Cue a phone call or a knock at the door. What might the caller/visitor want? A cup of sugar? A lift into town? Is it an old friend passing by? Or the postman with an important letter? You choose.

Whatever it is, you can use the new arrival as a way of 'lifting' the scene by injecting some unplanned activity or event. You might decide on a neighbour offering your main character a lift, allowing you to explain in dialogue between them a little more about what is going on and what emotions or concerns your main character is feeling. Using this as a jumping-off point, you might develop an extra strand to your storyline, where your character struggles to hide a secret from this nosy neighbour, adding to the tension. The possibilities are endless.

Remember, the newcomer can be as fleeting or as permanent as you wish, a walk-on part or a stayer. As long as they serve a useful purpose. It's your story, after all, and you can do whatever you want. God-like? You betcha.

Whatever their status or role, their arrival does not have to change the story in a big way. It's a device, pure and simple. What it should do is to give *you* a fresh perspective at a time when maybe your storyline is getting bogged down, and inject a whole new line of thought.

There are a few points to consider when bringing in someone new, no matter how briefly. What effect could he have on the scene? What could be the reaction to this newcomer, and how might it impact on the story? Could this introduction change certain events, thereby altering the flow of your story? Might the newcomer – as happened to me once – grow from a planned walk-on part only, to become a vital part of the story? And the main one is: can the new character add an extra exciting element to the plot and your writing?

TOP TIPS

- Choose a character at random and bring him (or her) in. Then think about the action and reaction.

- Think of him as a catalyst to something – anything – even in a small way.

- Use him to spur your main character(s) into thinking or acting in a way which adds extra vim or surprise to the story.

- Make sure he 'fits' the scene, no matter how briefly, and doesn't appear as a cut-and-paste job.

Don't write yourself short

A DILEMMA COMMON TO many writers is one of size – and I don't mean of screen, hard drive or their latest advance. I'm talking about the newly completed novel. It's a belter, with fantastic characters, plenty of action and love interest, and the ending is a corker. Frankly, Spielberg would hyperventilate if only he knew it was out there.

The only problem is, it's not long enough. Instead of being 90,000 words long, which the market might demand, it comes out at a rather wussy 60,000.

It's like being made to wear shorts as a kid – they might have pockets and a zip, even creases down the front, but they're still not *real* trousers.

So, how do you go about making a short book into a longer one without simply padding it to blazes?

To begin with, if you are convinced about the strength of your work, that it has 'legs' – in other words, it's more than just a short story – you have to take a serious look at what makes it so good in the first place. Is it the theme? The power of the characters? The pace and tone of the storyline? The timing or relevance for the market? Could it compete with other books out there (assuming it catches and holds an agent's or publisher's attention)? And do you have such a genuine conviction about it that you can't bear to chuck it in a drawer and forget it?

If so, then you have to look at ways in which you can use what you've got, and build on it.

It may end up bigger, as the actress said to the bishop, but will it be better?

First you have to step back from what you've written and look at how and where it could be expanded upon in a way that capitalises on its existing strengths. Don't forget, you're working with an already established storyline, and you don't want to change it out of all recognition or water it down. Any scenes added must enhance the story and give it more depth. Similarly, whatever characters you bring in must add to the existing cast in a relevant way, rather than simply cluttering up the place like discount night at the local bathhouse.

Could the storyline stand a second strand or a sub-plot, strongly related to the main events but coming from another start-point? This would allow you to bring in other points of view, with characters coming together later in the story. In each case, you have to stitch the new elements into the back-story so that they are not seen as a bolt-on simply to fill out the pages.

Be warned, though: once you start adding depth, character or new strands, the word count will grow – often alarmingly. It takes discipline and careful editing to control it, but as long as your new characters or scenes don't assume a greater significance than your original, or skew the story out of shape, it can be done.

Like how? I hear you ask. Taking an example right off the wall, let's say you have completed a book based on the Titanic. Unlike the ship, however, your book isn't big enough. It's actually more of a dinghy. It needs more size, more content, more oomph. You can't add more description, because there's plenty already and anyway, describing heaving open seas (or bosoms) can be boring. More dances and events are simply colour, you've covered all the on-board relationships adequately, so more of same would be gilding the lily. This is a dramatic tale, not an advert.

If the story is about a huge ship's invulnerability, you might have already covered the enormous iceberg or some other unexpected disaster which is going to befall this leviathan (now there's a word I never expected to use in print). Big ship full of bright souls versus even bigger, unstoppable object equals drama. But what about bringing in another human aspect?

For example, the engineer who built the ship. Was he working to required specifications, or had he been forced to skip some details here and there on grounds of cost? Was the original steel supplied of the right quality – and is there someone, somewhere who knows otherwise? Is there somebody with a long-term plan who wants to damage the ship mid-voyage for various reasons, but goes too far – with disastrous results? Any or all of these could be fed into the mix – along with their back-stories, of course.

In effect, what this is doing is introducing other characters who are as closely connected to the ship as those on board (perhaps they are even on board, too, and therefore suddenly pitched into a nightmare of their own making).

This new cast of characters allows a greater exploration of the build-up to the event, introducing more depth and more points of view to what in real life was a very human drama.

TOP TIPS

- Bigger is not automatically better. Additional material has to fit in with and improve the overall work.

- Analyse which parts of your existing work could benefit from extra emphasis, characters or scenes.

- Weaving in another strand can add depth and contrast, as well as giving an alternative point of view.

- Avoid padding, such as unnecessary adjectives, adverbs or birds in the trees.

The wave effect

I WAS ASKED RECENTLY how to judge the balance of a story, placing description versus action. In other words, how to avoid warbling on a bit too much about the leaves on the trees or the texture of a person's skin, rather than getting down to the exciting bits like emotion, action, conflict and all that good, gory stuff.

Each story is different, of course, and balance isn't something you can set in advance, like bass and treble on a hi-fi system. You can plan, certainly, but most plans vary to one degree or another as the storyline develops. For example, you cannot easily say, well, I'll have ten lines of nice descriptive prose, followed by fifteen lines of a chase scene, followed by a bit more prose, a bit of lovey-dovey stuff, followed by ...

That would become so formulaic and unrealistic as to render the story unbalanced rather than the other way round.

As in real life, nothing is a flat line; there are ups and downs all the time. It's akin to waves in the sea – with peaks and troughs making for a fascinating, varied outlook, where you wait to see what happens next. Compare this to a motionless lake, which may be scenic, even calming, for a while, but after a bit, you want to see something happening ... unless you happen to be alongside Loch Ness and have an over-imaginative frame of mind.

The fact is that a story cannot remain on a single level throughout. Too much low and it becomes boring and static – and readers begin skimming to the good bits; too much high and it leaves little room for plot or character development and background setting. Either way, the story needs to move in order to capture the reader.

Troughs. These might be compared to the descriptive

narrative – the part dealing with setting, characters and background. This doesn't mean boring, because setting and character is important to give background and realism to people and place, and allows us to build a picture for the reader.

Undercurrents. These are the underbelly of the story, sitting quietly but ready to burst through to the surface. These undercurrents, by their nature, are turbulent and dangerous, waiting to catch the unwary.

Slopes. The part dealing with the build-up of emotion, setting the scene for impending action, the raising of tension as a key plot-piece unfolds and the protagonists prepare to meet danger and conflict.

Peaks. Finally, sitting at the crest of the waves, come the fast-moving, unpredictable white caps, where we encounter the heights of tension and action, either on a physical or emotional level, which carry readers along, past their bed-time … or past their train stop, as has happened to me on a couple of occasions.

But while a story can be exciting from start to finish, it can't reasonably stay on an unrelenting high. The reader needs an occasional break, otherwise the pitch of tension can lose its edge … and, pretty soon, you're in danger of losing your reader.

Thus, on the other side of the wave, we allow the tension to slide a little, letting the reader gather breath before the next build-up, the next burst of action or drama.

Again, you cannot prepare a formula for this wave effect, because, more often than not, this is determined by the pace of your story. What you can do is check your writing as you go, to see if you have spent too long on either a high or a low.

A simple, visual way of doing this is to draw a flat line across a piece of paper (or the living-room wall if your partner has an unusually forbearing nature), marking off points at intervals. These become, in effect, the markers of your story – the points at which you have a peak or a trough in the storyline. The first marker would be chapter one, where your main characters might first meet, for example. Depending on how you want to open the story, this would be on or above the line. If you decide on a low-tempo encounter, your marker would sit on the line and be headed 'A&B meet', with start-to-end page numbers as a running guide. The next marker might be the introduction of the villain of the piece. This would be on or slightly above the line, to show a rise in tension or conflict. Thus each marker would represent highs or lows according to the flow and pace of your story, in effect charting the waves throughout – and giving you a quick visual check of how your plot is unfolding as you go. It will also allow you to go straight to a page number if further editing is needed, without searching through your manuscript for the appropriate section or paragraph.

The wave pattern, incidentally, might change as you re-work the story and either insert or take out a particular scene or event. But the one thing this visual check does allow you to do is to keep an eye on the ups and downs of your plot, and ensure you don't get stuck in the doldrums.

TOP TIPS

- Varying the pace keeps the reader interested – and makes the writing fun.

- A line of markers allows you to scan the ups and downs of your story.

- Don't ignore the undercurrents, part of the build-up to action and tension.

- If the writing excites you, think what it will do for the reader.

You as a Writer

WRITERS ARE NOT MACHINES. We need to think about what we want to write, how we want to do it … and what we're trying to achieve.

A woman once asked me, 'Do writers have to be a little eccentric?'

'No,' I replied. 'But it usually helps.'

You as a Writer (continued)

Just for the record

A QUESTION THAT OCCURS to many aspiring writers is the thorny one of credibility. It usually goes like: 'I haven't written much, so will my lack of a track record count against me?' This concern that a distant editor will not take them seriously unless they can demonstrate previously published work is very real.

However, the simple answer is that you can't do much about it at this stage of your writing career, so don't worry. But you can overcome it.

As a general rule, unless you are writing an authoritative non-fiction piece where a recognised degree of expertise is required to add weight to the article, the question of track record should count somewhat less than the article or story itself. As far as fiction is concerned, most editors are interested in the story content, not whether you can fill a whole shelf of the British Library with your back-catalogue.

Pieces are rejected all the time for all kinds of reasons; wrong target market, poor quality writing, repetition, lack of 'spark', editor's toothache on a wet Monday. But while a known author might have a degree of edge in the initial reading stages over a complete unknown, there is so much demand for fresh content that unknowns get their first acceptance letter every day of the week (and, if you need some consolation, 'knowns' get their fair share of rejections, too).

This might add weight to the suspicion among many writers that publishers don't know what they want until they see it. Given the shifting nature of readers' interests, this suspicion is not entirely without foundation.

But, instead of a disadvantage, this should be seen as good news for writers everywhere. A changing market means it is ripe for trying out new topics. Even tapping into a known subject with an entirely fresh approach will often catch an editor's eye, whereas a weary piece following a well-trodden path will whistle off the desk into the 'not this one' file quicker than a fried egg off a greasy plate.

With non-fiction, it is important to present an accurate, well-researched and interesting piece which shows you have a good grasp of your subject matter. If you can also claim some familiarity or connection with the topic, then you should let the editor know in your covering letter, even if it is your first piece. A well-written inside track often beats an outside observer hands down. If, on the other hand, all you have is an interest purely to get the piece written and sold, then you can only let your writing speak for you. In either case it is worth repeating that a selection of good-quality photos to back up your feature will stand a better chance of catching an editorial eye than a page of text by itself, because, if the editor does not have to source photos, it saves time and money (and you get paid for supplying them instead).

With fiction, it is the story that counts. Yes, a known name below the title will stand out to begin with, but the writing is the main decider. And this is where you are on your own, with only your skill as a story-teller to get you through.

So, with such a stacked deck against you, what can you do?

Well, you can open with a bang, for a start. Let that first line stand out by making it a belter. DON'T have your story beginning with a whole page of solid, stodgy text – it's an entertainment, not an instruction manual in a tractor factory. Put in some dialogue, keep the paragraphs short and snappy, make the whole page look lively and interesting, and if you can use a seasonal slant, that will also help. Bear in mind that your text will appear in narrow columns on the magazine page, so you need to break it up to take account of this.

Try introducing some humour in your dialogue. Very few conversations in life (unless they involve a divorce court or a dismissal letter) are devoid of humour, and there is no reason why your writing should not reflect this. It need not be a string of jokes, but humour can be indicated by the dialogue, mannerisms or reactions of your characters. In fact, if you find your characters actually taking over to the extent that they begin to say or do things you had not planned (no, you're not in the twilight zone, I promise – it does happen), then let them; it will probably seem more natural.

Your first 'sale', of course, once made, is a huge leap. And having achieved that acceptance and with the printed words on the page to prove it, you can now demonstrate that you have done it – a great morale booster for the future.

Until then, all you can do is turn in the most professional, accurate and entertaining pieces you can write. Note the plural: *never* sit back and wait to see what one piece produces. Get on with the next project. And be ready to work on each piece more than once, possibly re-working them along the way to suit the next market you submit to.

It's what writers do.

TOP TIPS

- The only way to build a writing track record is by doing it.

- The market needs content, ideas and, above all, submissions.

- Be reliable, professional, and on time. A solid reputation counts.

- Finish one project, start another. It's called writing.

Find the write you

IF YOU'VE EVER TRIED to hum a certain tune, only to find yourself straying into an entirely different, but not dissimilar, melody, you will know how difficult it is to get the old one out of your head.

The same feeling of confusion is occasionally experienced – albeit in a different way – by writers who have become immersed in another writer's style, to the extent that their own work begins to take on similarities, however unintentionally. This is a common phenomenon for editors who receive manuscripts that are little more than a pale imitation of a (usually) well-known author's style. They aren't all jumping on a bandwagon and hoping to get published because a particular style or genre is in vogue; some are by writers who have not yet discovered their own style. And while imitation might be the sincerest form of flattery, new writers need to work hard to avoid this pitfall.

So how do writers discover their own style of writing which sets them apart from the rest of the herd?

Well, subject matter is a fairly good start. What do you want to write about? Crime? Romance? Horror? Sci-Fi? Humour? (The same question, incidentally, applies equally to short, as well as long fiction, *and* non-fiction). Publishers are always saying they are looking for something 'new' or 'fresh'. However, pin them to the wall with a cocktail stick and ask them what that is, and they probably won't be able to tell you. Irritating, isn't it? But a safe bet is that, the elusive 'new' or 'fresh' *won't* be a re-hash of the same thing currently filling the shelves of your local bookshop. Of course, you will continue to see plenty of look-alikes of the latest bestseller, and ask yourself why you shouldn't try them, too. But remember, by the time you see these in the shops, they will have been written over a year before, so you've already missed the boat.

The simple answer is to look for something that is not currently covered. Aim for characters (fiction) which are new, and settings or subjects (non-fiction) which have not been done to death already.

The best way to do this (apart from reading voraciously, of course, which is a must) is to study the market. Spend time in your bookshop and newsagent, and look at the current favourites. While you are at it, analyse what it is about a favoured author that makes him or her so popular or enjoyable. Look at other authors and see how they differ. What attracts you to a particular writer? Is it the plot? Characterisation? Subject matter? Language? Consider the structure; the length of sentences; the economy (or eloquence) of style; the use of humour or tension.

Viewpoint is another consideration, because this may well have a dramatic effect on the way you write. Some writers can only write in the first person, with styles varying from the terse, no-nonsense 'private eye' genre of writing, to the elegant, descriptive and personal prose of, say, historical fiction. Others prefer third person or even multiple viewpoints, which allow more freedom of expression and 'angles' to a story.

If you are not sure what suits you, then experiment; try all of them until you feel comfortable in the results you achieve. One way to do this is to take a paragraph at random from a book. If it's in first person, re-write it in third. If lengthy and descriptive, pare it right down to see where you can economise, while keeping the sense of what is being said. If the style is 'tight', add to it to flesh it out slightly, and see how – or if – it changes. Then look honestly at what you've written and see if you have either improved it (to your own tastes) or not.

Another useful way of experimenting is to choose two or three competitions and write something to order. The organisers – especially in *Writers' News* – often set a specific theme, which will force you to consider a story you might not normally attempt. This in turn will make you approach the task with a change of style. The rules may also stipulate a strict word-length, requiring the writing to be tightly controlled (great discipline for magazine writing, this), which brings its own style and structure, too. Others may well give you the first or last line to be used, and it is not unknown for competition rules to specify a viewpoint or a particular setting … all of which will make you think outside your normal square.

Using these exercises, you may find yourself attracted to one style because you feel comfortable with the way it progresses, rejecting others because they simply don't suit you. This is fine; whatever some people may imply, writing is not meant to be endured, like lying on a bed of nails or sticking hot needles in your eyeballs. It's supposed to be enjoyable! And you *are* allowed to be pleased with what you've written.

And finally, if a passage sounds pretty good, it usually is, so as a last test, why not read (and record) what you have written, to see if the words flow off the page as easily as they may have flown on to it.

You never know, while you're at it, you may discover you have another talent!

TOP TIPS

- Decide what *you* want to write and work at it.

- Find what writing viewpoint sounds comfortable for you.

- Study your writing strengths and weaknesses.

- Don't be a pale imitation of someone else.

You as a Writer (continued)

Who do you write for?

A SUBJECT WHICH OCCASIONALLY pops up whenever writers gather together in furtive huddles and talk about the art of putting words on paper, is 'writing for a market'. Now, if you're new to the business and taking your first tentative steps on to the page, so to speak, this won't mean much. You may, after all, still be wondering where the heck the market is, let alone trying to write for it.

The term simply means aiming a feature, story or book at a specific type of publication or genre, depending on readers' interests. Thus, a short story featuring love and romance would mainly find a home in women's magazines, since that is the biggest – and most voracious – market. Equally, a non-fiction piece about cars would generally be best targeted at one of the motoring publications. (That said, depending on the slant given, it might also be of interest to other publications where a specific element of that same story – perhaps the personal experience of the writer – could make it more of a general-interest piece).

With magazines, the most important thing is to study their writers' guidelines. These will tell you how many words to use, the style to follow, the 'do nots' as well as the 'dos', and even how to submit your piece. Ignore these basic requirements and the editor will likely have an attack of the vapours and set fire to your manuscript.

It makes absolute sense for anyone trying to make a commercial go of their work to get used to writing for a market in this way. They may, after a while and a few acceptances under their belt, find themselves being commissioned to write more, ending up concentrating on a specialised market for which they feel comfortable writing.

Penning novels is somewhat less precise. With magazines,

because of the relatively shorter time-lag between submission and publication, it is perhaps less likely for trends or topics to have changed suddenly, rendering the piece dated.

Books, however, are like pregnant elephants – they go through a lengthy gestation period accompanied by much roaring and fuss. They take longer to sell, edit and publish, and may finally hit the bookshops anything up to two years after acceptance. Many an eager writer has taken note of what is currently 'hot' in the best-seller lists and rushed home to feverishly thrash out his version, convinced of sure-fire success, only to find at the end that tastes have moved on and everyone is going bananas about something else entirely.

It's essential for any writer to keep an eye on what is selling, whether producing a 1,000-word story or a book of 90,000 words. Choose a topic which hasn't been in vogue since papyrus was the big thing, and you're wasting your time. Magazines cannot use them, agents can't place them with publishers and bookshops may have a problem categorising them. And in this compartmentalised world, like it or not, if something can't easily be labelled, it may be all too quickly ignored.

In effect, these are basic market rules that are as old as the hills. As Confucius might have said: *He who loads barrow with stuff nobody wants is dumb bunny.*

The only way round this is to study your target market. Haunt the racks in newsagents, browse the bookshops and see what is in vogue. Find out what sells and you stand a better chance of success than simply pitching any old story into an envelope and hoping for the best.

There was a time eons ago when I used to write stories I knew my mother would like. Not as weird as you might think, because my mother used to inhale magazine fiction, and it seemed like a good idea at the time. It was also a great training ground.

Note that I did *not* run my stories past her first (early experience showed it merely led to doting smiles and being told to finish my tea). But I knew what subjects she liked and sometimes used her as a sounding board (until she turned to reading hospital stories, in which I had no interest whatsoever).

And this leads neatly on to an important proviso: you should not write something that goes against your instincts, or about which you don't feel comfortable. If romantic stories are what float your boat, then why not stick with what you know? If you prefer reading crime or fantasy novels, and are comfortable with the terminology, pace and style, then go with them.

In essence, along with studying a market or genre, you first have to please yourself. If you aren't happy with what you've written, ten pence to a pound of old slippers, neither will the editors or readers. And you should *enjoy* what you're putting on the page, because, if you like it, it will have a more genuine – and fresher – feel than if you're writing about something in which you have no real interest. Equally, creating characters you don't really like will come across as cardboard cut-outs, lacking depth.

They say it's a poor comic who laughs at his own jokes. But I take the view that if I'm not pleased with what I've written, why should anyone else be? Yes, most of us will feel at some stage that we could have structured something better, or approached a story from a different viewpoint and so on. But that's the learning process, and how we become better writers.

TOP TIPS

- Ask yourself what market you would like to write for. Having a focus is a huge help.

- Writing against your instincts can be frustrating and off-putting.

- Try to be pleased with what you have written.

- Have fun with your writing – suffering is not an essential element.

You as a Writer (continued)

Writing for pleasure or profit

WHILE TALKING TO A group of writers a while back about submitting their work to various paying markets, one member approached me rather challengingly and said, 'What about writers who only do it for pleasure, then, not profit?'

(The way he said 'profit' made it clear that anyone who sold their writing was a step up from a swamp creature, but marginally lower than those quiffed photographers who used to patrol seaside resorts with an empty camera and a fistful of blank receipts).

I can't recall what I said at the time. It was probably no different to what I would say now, which is 'Well, what about them?'

There are gazillions of people out there who write solely for their own pleasure, be it for the joy of constructing a story from nothing, the satisfaction of playing with words on paper, or even recording their own or their family history and experiences for no other reason than that they want to. And logic says there must be some brilliant writers among them.

But they're not a special breed (as the gentleman seemed to imply); nor are they elitists to be spoken of in reverent tones. (No more, I hasten to add, are writers wot sell their work, before anyone gets the wrong idea.)

All writers do so *mainly* for pleasure. How else – and why – would we do it otherwise? Most will admit to feeling some level of satisfaction at what they accomplish, be it poetry, stories or articles, whether languishing on their computer, at the bottom of the sock drawer or in a plastic bag behind the wardrobe. In such a solitary and inward-looking pursuit, there has to be an element of enjoyment, otherwise you might as well go out and tear hubcaps off passing cars.

However, some – perhaps most – writers like to think that what they do isn't half bad and are confident enough to submit their work in the hope that an editor will like what they've done and pay them a sum of money for the privilege.

They may be members of writers groups, they may not. Whatever their standing, they write with a goal in mind ... that one day they will get that fantastic acceptance letter and be allowed to walk around on a cloud for several days afterwards or haunt their local newsagent like Marley's ghost until the magazine is published.

However, in the same way that this desire or eventual success should never lead published and hope-to-be-published scribes to look down on others who never submit anything anywhere, there is no shame in feeling the opposite – that niggling urge to send a story to a magazine to see what happens.

DON'T feel guilty at the thought of wanting to see your work in print.

DON'T be put off by doubts of yielding to the pull of the commercial world, the tawdry (don't you love that word?) attraction of possibly getting a cheque in the post and of scarpering down to the shop to buy 100 copies of the magazine when it comes out. (And yes, gentle reader, that does happen – I know because ...).

Look at it like this: you've put in a lot of hard work and effort, perhaps over several drafts and re-writes, maybe struggling with detail versus storyline and fighting for precious moments in your day to add a few words here and there. You've ignored the comments of friends or family – many of whom don't really understand, let's face it – and continued pursuing your goal regardless.

Because you want to.

In short, you've created something very rare. Why so? Well, unless you're an out-and-out plagiarist, who gets fun copying stuff from books, you've created something unique to *you*. And you should be proud of that fact. You should at least allow yourself to feel some satisfaction (albeit not so much so that you can't get through an average-size doorway afterwards).

Another however: *if* you start to get that itch, that niggling feeling, that urgent voice saying, *I wonder if this is good enough*, it's perfectly natural and healthy. You're allowed. It's your creation, and you can send it off if you want to. Or not.

Personally, I feel that if you honestly think it's as good as or better than other stories or articles you've read in magazines, then you should give it a go.

It's not vanity, nor is it cheapening what you do. It's a perfectly normal extension of the creative process. And if you think it might give pleasure to others, then why not share it?

And that is the nub of the thing. Whether paid for or not, what you have written might well be of interest to someone else. Be it fiction, poetry, article or personal history, you don't have to try and sell it if you don't want to. You might even consider making it available for free. At least then you might receive some useful and constructive comments which may help with future projects.

The important thing is, keep writing. And long may you derive much pleasure from it, whatever your goal.

TOP TIPS

- If you enjoy your writing, it will show through.

- There's no shame in wanting to be published.

- Even if you write purely for your own pleasure, having some feedback can be extremely helpful.

- Writing as a pursuit is great therapy.

You as a Writer (continued)

Believe in you

IT'S NOT UNUSUAL FOR people meeting famous writers they admire to say afterwards something like, 'He/ she was so *ordinary*!'

Now, whether there was a suspicion beforehand that said famed author might have a spare head tucked under their arm, or a silicon chip in place of a brain, I'm never sure. Ten to one it means the author was found to be surprisingly genial and down-to-earth, rather than so far up himself that light couldn't penetrate the surrounding darkness.

Ego – or lack of one – aside, it helps to reflect that successful writers (and how you measure success depends on you) are, for the most part, ordinary people. They breathe the same as everyone else, they survive the same daily rigours of life and, as my sainted old dad used to say about VIPs, they have to get out of the bath for a pee, the same as the rest of us.

So what's so special, then, that gets these other people published?

Let's ignore for the sake of our blood pressure, the celebrity writer. It's a fact of modern life, and pointless getting too worked up about people cashing in – or being shown *how* to cash in on their supposed fame by a smart agent/PR expert. It's like saying, 'If only I'd been born taller/thinner/blonder/smarter/faster than I am.'

It didn't happen, so suck it up.

(Actually, if I may confess a childhood wish here, I always wanted to be 6'2" tall. Don't ask me why – well, yes, I'll tell you why: my fictional hero, Simon 'The Saint' Templar was that height, so I figured, why not? Nonsense? Of course it was. But when you're only eight years old and 3' 6" on a bucket, it's allowed. Did I hang like a bat from doorways in the vain hope that I'd stretch a bit? Well, I tried it once, but succeeded in ripping the beading off the doorframe. The resultant lecture from my father convinced me that there are only certain things you can change. And ruining a perfectly good doorframe wasn't one of them.)

In other words, you have to make the most of what you've got.

In writing, success in getting published is usually down to luck, hard work, persistence and producing what the market wants.

But it also needs a hefty measure of self-belief.

I know a couple of people who will never drive a car as long as there are spots in front of their eyes. It's not because they're dim-witted or have the coordination of a mud puddle; it's because they simply don't believe they can do it.

Yet those same two people do all manner of other things in life without a second thought, purely because in their subconscious, they think – or assume – they can. No doubts, no lingering fears – they get on with it.

Looking up at successful authors and thinking 'I couldn't do that', can prove a real problem for some people. Lump on top of that all the other fears and self-doubts we're prone to from time to time, and it might become almost insurmountable.

But there are certain things you can do to put yourself in the right ballpark.

Write for the market. Recognising that there are things you can write which will probably *never* be published is one thing. In other words, produce what the market wants, thereby getting your foot on the ladder and building a track record. If, once you're there, you want to take a punt on writing something outside the mainstream, that's your choice. But you have to get your foot in the door first.

Be professional in your attitude and approach. Mavericks who write in green ink on both sides of the paper, then insist on phoning an editor the day after posting the manuscript to see if they've syndicated the idea around the English-speaking world without telling the author, are prone to disappointment. And yes, they do exist. Freelance writing is like any other job: treat it seriously and professionally, and the approach will usually be reciprocated. It still doesn't guarantee publication, but at least you'll be closer than otherwise. The alternative is like turning up for the office party wearing a creepy smile and a suit made of cling-film; it won't get you asked back.

Be prepared to write to order. Most writers try all manner of things along the way, be it poetry, short fiction, articles, comedy material or books. Much of it is to find out what they can or cannot do; others do it because they like to vary their output.

Don't be precious. Be prepared to accept criticism. Yes, it's your baby and you've spilled *blood* getting every creative word on paper. But if editors says they want changes, be prepared to listen and re-write. It might be the only chance you get.

Keep writing. Writing one story and sitting back to wait for results is a sure-fire way of getting old and disappointed. Write another, then another. Submit them and if they come back, review them and send them out to someone else. Activity breeds results and inspires more ideas.

Assume that everything is possible. Don't even give a moment's thought to doubt – or doubters. Nobody can guarantee you success, no more than added height, brains or beauty. But neither should you promote obstacles for yourself by thinking *I can't do that.*

TOP TIPS

- Believe in yourself and keep trying.

- Be professional – turn in the best work you can.

- Don't try to cut corners.

- Don't be precious about your work – be prepared to make changes if asked.

- Study the market and follow any guidelines.

You as a Writer (continued)

Passion or skill?

ASK WRITERS WHY THEY do it, and they'll sometimes tell you it's because they want to get published. Some will say they simply have a desire to write. Others will describe it as an itch which has to be scratched, or the fulfilment of a long-held dream to create something and see it put down on paper. The short answer is, some do it for pleasure, others for profit, but most, if honest, will admit they do it for both.

Whatever your reasons, there has to be a measure of both passion and skill in what you do to bring out your best writing, and to help those words flow in a coherent and attractive way. With luck, you will never run out of either.

Speaking personally, when I'm away from my keyboard for any length of time, I've been known to get ever so slightly cranky. This will come as a startling revelation to my friends and family, but it's true. Of course, I disguise this with consummate skill and nobody realises it. The fact is that I can't wait to get back to work on my current project, whether it's a book, short story or feature. But there have been times – fortunately, very few – when, for some reason, I haven't experienced that same excitement about a piece I've been working on. I take this as a bad sign, because it means I don't feel committed about what I'm doing and am subconsciously putting it off. (DIY, worming the cat and filling in my tax returns have much the same effect).

I invariably get round this lack of enthusiasm by recognising that something isn't working and starting again, or by changing the direction or focus of the project until I regain that missing thrill. Often I will drop what I'm struggling with and work on something else until I can see more clearly what I need to do. The recognition signal is that I once again get a buzz and can't wait to finish it.

Passion, desire, call it what you will, is probably what motivates most writers at heart; the passion to invent characters and scenes, to weave plots and stories peppered with twists and thrills; to strive to portray accurately what we see in our minds in a way that rings true to the reader. The same motivation helps create believable protagonists that leap off the page, to give them that touch of reality that takes them beyond being cardboard figures with no attraction for the reader. Passion can also help keep us focussed – sometimes to a level where friends and family may think we've taken leave of the planet.

Most of all, passion is what keeps us going, through bad-hair days, bad writing days, and days when rejections slips pile up and brown envelopes keep winging their way back home like sorry, bedraggled pigeons. Passion keeps us believing that one day we'll receive a kindly letter saying: *Yes, we'll take it.*

Passion makes us read, too. For without reading, we cannot aspire to equal or even hope to better what we admire in others.

But passion, as the actress once said to the poor old bishop, is not always enough; you need a bit of skill, too. With all the desire in the world, if you have none of the basic skills (we're back to writing, here, by the way) you are going to waste a lot of time, effort and emotional energy.

Some very skilful writers are not necessarily good at producing good page-turners. Over the years, many successful journalists have failed to make the grade as novelists. Whether this is due to a lack of passion is debatable, but nobody would argue that their writing skills are there in abundance. For some reason, the way they use them in their normal work doesn't quite work in another.

Skills, of course, can be acquired or learnt. Courses and workshops will help with plotting, characterisation, structure, layout, presentation – the elements of building a story from start to finish. Skills will provide the framework on which a story can be hung, allowing you to put the whole work together in a presentable format that is acceptable to readers and makes them want to keep reading.

Naturally, there are writers who demonstrate special skills

which owe more to something almost magical than mere nuts-and-bolts writing techniques. They have the qualities as described above (and probably passion in spades), but they also possess that extra something which allows them to do things with a storyline that other writers cannot do in quite the same way.

However, if we lesser mortals concentrate on the learnable skills, adding them to the passion we feel for writing and the desire to be published, we may also achieve great things.

Passion can propel us to snatch a vital few minutes out of a busy day, to write another paragraph or two.

Passion will help us sacrifice other leisure pursuits in favour of putting down on paper what is bursting to get out.

Skill helps us feed in that paragraph in such a way that it enhances the story rather than being just another bunch of words that have no place or meaning.

Skill will help us recognise that, occasionally, what we have written isn't that great, and should be left out or ruthlessly edited, otherwise it will spoil the whole story.

TOP TIPS

- If you have passion for your writing, it will show through.

- Skills can be learned, and will pay off in the end.

- Passion will help you through the awkward moments and propel you forward.

- Skill will help you write in a way to suit a specific market.

The story-teller's apprentice

A PLUMBER FRIEND OF mine was recently talking about when he started out in the profession many years ago. He began as an apprentice – what in some trades is known unbecomingly as 'an oily rag' – to an experienced plumber. This introduction to the noble art of plumbing meant he was given all the fetch-and-carry jobs, such as running off every few minutes for whatever materials were needed (including a one-way pipe and a long stand), digging trenches, boring holes … basically, whatever the plumber required him to do. One of the worst jobs, which he hated due to suffering mild claustrophobia, was clambering about in gloomy lofts.

In time, naturally, he realised something the plumber hadn't told him: that all these 'apprentice' jobs were really just a run-up – a taster – to the real work, and that whatever he learned as a beginner would stand him in good stead. Because while he might not like fetching and carrying, or crawling about in confined spaces on his hands and knees, it would soon become second nature. And, as well as being instructed formally where all the pipes went so that the system worked efficiently, he was learning subliminally, too.

You can probably see where I'm going with this.

I've met quite a few writers who have launched into their very first book without actually putting pen to paper in any other way. No short stories, no articles – probably not even a letter home to dear old Mum. So far, I haven't personally met one for whom it has worked.

I'm sure they are out there, of course. I'm not saying it's impossible – merely unusual. But for most writers, it's not that simple.

One way or another, you have to do an apprenticeship.

But why?

Well, like the plumber's apprentice, you learn more about any craft simply by doing it. And even though a lot of what you do might appear mundane, even uninspiring (and we all go through that, believe me), there's no beating getting in at the sharp end. Because while you're plugging away, you are beginning to absorb skills, habits and knowledge about the art without thinking about it. And, in doing so, you are learning how to assemble all the requirements for making a story come together.

Doing the groundwork. Like the apprentice, you have to make sure everything is ready before you begin. Yes, in writing, you can do some research as you go. But the job is so much easier if you don't have to keep breaking off in mid-flow, thus spoiling your concentration.

Pacing yourself. You may be desperate to finish a scene or story. This could be because of time constraints, or because the sheer excitement of a good scene threatens to take over. And while this is a wonderful feeling for any writer, you have to learn to temper your enthusiasm and not splurge out the ending all in one go. To do so might ruin what should have been a gradual build-up of tension. The main rule is, don't cut corners, no matter how tempting.

Alternative routes. Occasionally, you may find yourself up against a brick wall with no easy way through. Learn to look for an alternative, instead of automatically junking the whole thing (although that, too, might be an option you have to consider). Essentially, find out what works for you, and it will stand you in good stead for the future.

Having enough material. The story must have legs – not padding. Have you got the storyline, plot, characters and scenes to last? Or will you run out of material halfway through? Building a synopsis or chapter plan might help here – as will experience.

Quality control. Unlike the poor apprentice, you won't have a plumber looking over your shoulder. But if you can develop a critical eye for your *own* work (most easily learnt through analysing what you like about other writers) you will find yourself checking your output as you go, thus avoiding some of the more obvious mistakes.

Pride in your work. This should be a natural development, because everybody likes to think they're getting better as they go along. The more you write, one hopes, the more you improve.

Learning to take criticism. Whether it comes in the shape of a refusal letter from an editor or the comments of a writing tutor, it's something all writers have to face. And like the weary apprentice, after a hard day slaving over a U-bend, being told something isn't right can be depressing. But that's all it is; it means it's not right. So fix it. Even if you do decide to junk it and start again.

Stretching yourself. Don't settle for the easy jobs. If you only ever write short stories aimed at magazines, enter competitions once in a while. Try a non-fiction project. It might not be what you want to do all the time, but working on something different, with different demands, can be a useful challenge.

Don't hide in the attic. Like the apprentice hoping that if the plumber can't find him, he won't be landed with another job, keeping your writing to yourself won't help you grow. Get it out there. Submit it to magazines or show it to writing group members and friends. Good or bad, feedback is essential if you want to know – and learn by – what others think of your writing.

TOP TIPS

- Like any other job or craft, writing has a learning curve. This is best served by doing it.

- Learn the rules of market guidelines and presentation, and you will move forward a lot faster.

- Be professional in your presentation, language and attention to detail.

- Study your competitors and analyse how they do it.
- If offered advice, accept it and learn from it.

You as a Writer (continued)

Put on your purple hat

THERE'S A WELL-KNOWN poem which has been around for some time, known variously as *The Ages of Woman ...* or simply, The Purple Hat poem. It deals with how a woman sees herself throughout her life. Starting at age 3, she sees herself as a queen, then as Cinderella ... and runs all the way up to 80, when, after a life of living by the rules, she puts on a purple hat and says to hell with all of you, I'm off to enjoy myself. (I'm paraphrasing here, so please don't write and tell me off.)

Now, I know a lot of you out there are of the hairy male persuasion, and wouldn't dream of putting on anything purple unless you were (a) aspiring to the priesthood or (b) pushing your luck on the fashion front. But bear with me, because this applies to you, too.

Writing is all about rules, and mostly, if we want to be proficient writers, we follow them carefully; use commas here, speech-marks there, write for the market, double-space your manuscript, use one point of view at a time, etc and so forth. All good stuff and not to be ignored if you wish to be taken seriously as a professional writer.

But every now and then, don't you think you should let go a bit or, as my dear old mum used to say, let out your girdle (or belt, if you're a bloke) and live a little?

There are solid reasons for doing this. Firstly, rules can sometimes stifle our inner creativity. Yes, they're important in the normal course of events, but every once in a while, foregoing them is like walking on to a beach, kicking off your shoes, rolling up your trousers and flexing your toes in the water. It's liberating.

Another reason to kick the rules into the long grass occasionally is to see what we're capable of when we're not following them. I don't mean *Lord of the Flies* kind of stuff – we're civilised, after all, not a bunch of beasts. But have you ever tried writing something … *daring*? Something you wouldn't normally write?

I remember once being on Dartmoor with school friends at the age of 12, and being aware that nobody else was about. By nobody, I mean ADULTS. (We were on summer camp and the teachers had left us to put up the tents while they went to the pub.) And there was all this *space* and no-one filling it who could tell us what to do.

Best of all, there was an absolute blinder of an echo, which we only became aware of when knocking in the tent pegs and finding the *tock* noise coming back at us.

So we started shouting. And whistling. And making daft noises. Hell, we were boys – what do you expect?

Then someone bellowed a swear-word.

Cue giggles and scanning the horizon to see if anyone in authority was about, and, within seconds, the harmless rolling slopes of Dartmoor – and a few hairy cows – were being roundly abused with every rude word a bunch of 12-year-olds could hurl at them … and quite a few we only *thought* were rude, but weren't sure about. And every word came winging straight back. Have you ever been sworn at by your own echo? *It's brilliant!*

Anyway, the thing was, after weeks and months of following rules of every description, we were suddenly free to do what we'd always wanted, but had never had the time or the opportunity to do.

It was bloody marvellous.

But have you ever tried writing something you wouldn't normally write? (And I don't mean taking a spray can and writing *I WOZ 'ERE* all over the nearest railway carriage.) I mean writing something you don't even read. Wedded to Romance? Try Crime. Chuckling at humour? Take a walk on the Dark Side. Thrilled with mysteries? Let your mind go off into Sci-Fi. Grounded with the everyday? Take off into Fantasy.

A case in point recently was when I met a librarian friend who admitted she had tried writing erotica. Just to see if she could. She admitted it was difficult at first, purely because it wasn't something she'd ever dreamed of writing. She even felt a bit … naughty.

But liberated.

She didn't actually show me what she had written, but when she went back to her usual writing style (relationships and crime), she felt as if she had taken a real break, and was able to launch herself back into her work with renewed enthusiasm.

I usually swap between non-fiction, features, relationship fiction, crime thrillers and letters to my MP. And that, for me, offers a broad enough scope which lets me ring the changes and get a fresh perspective on whatever comes next. But I know through experience that dipping the writing toe into uncharted waters can unleash a whole new approach.

So, if you're feeling a little constrained, why not put on *your* purple hat (real or otherwise) and go 'out' there once in a while. Defy convention and write something completely different. See what happens.

You never know, you might just surprise yourself.

TOP TIPS

- Choose a genre you don't normally write – and go for it.

- Take a cue from television or film, and write something in the same style.

- Don't worry about your usual locations or characters – get wild!

- Try to write with a smile on your face.

Be an active writer

A LESSON I LEARNED a long time ago was that activity is the key to most things. The more you do, the more you achieve. Not that rushing around like a chicken with two heads will necessarily breed success, but neither will too much navel-gazing about the art of writing (although it does have its place). It's rather a question of making sure the activity you undertake is (a) focussed and (b) has a point other than simply bashing away on a keyboard and hoping you get lucky.

So let's take a pause from the mechanics of putting words on paper for a few minutes, and see how activity in writing generally can help you further your aims.

First of all, let's take it as read that you are not a one-story wonder, with a single piece in you before the muse shuts down and goes into permanent hibernation. Assume, rather, that there is a veritable torrent of ideas inside you waiting to be unleashed … if only you had the time to do it. Welcome to the club, because that's how most writers are. It's why so many of us carry notebooks or recorders; if we're not actually *thinking* about writing, jotting down ideas or noting overheard snippets of conversation because they may be useful sometime, then it's only because we're hard at work trying to fashion those thoughts, ideas and notes into something coherent … and therefore saleable.

Every writing project should, ideally, have a natural time span. Whether it takes a day, week, month or years to complete doesn't matter – it should have an end in sight somewhere, because without that idea of completion, you'll never truly let go of it. And you need to, in order to see it through and get on with all those other ideas bursting to get out of your head. True, you can put down one project and work on something else, but in your own mind at least, you should discipline yourself to finish each job – eventually.

Once you have done this, and have got it out of the way (with luck, heading for an editor's desk) GET ON WITH THE NEXT ONE!

Ideally again, a useful habit to develop is of working on more than one project at a time – or at least having notes in hand about future writing plans and projects. The reason is that if you happen to run dry on one, switching to another may allow your thoughts to flow more easily. Whether short stories, non-fiction or book-length works, there should never be a point at which you don't have a fairly solid idea of what you intend to work on next.

This ongoing activity serves three main purposes: the first is that waiting for the postman is simply counter-productive and depressing; you gain an intimate knowledge of the sound of your postman's footsteps and how much junk mail comes through your letterbox, but that's all. The second is that even when you make a sale, it can take months to come through – months when you should be working on something else rather than letting your writing 'muscles' go to waste. The third is one of morale: the more work you complete, the more projects you have out there, the easier it becomes to widen and vary your writing as those ideas start to flow on to the page rather than simply sitting on a notepad or churning around inside your brain. In other words, the activity of writing truly becomes part of your everyday life, each project potentially acting as a springboard to another idea, whether for the same market or an entirely different one. This springboard effect is particularly important if an editor likes what you have done and asks to see more. There's nothing worse than being asked for more ideas and having to admit that you hadn't thought beyond the last writing session.

The other side – some say the routine, boring side – to being a productive writer, is actually recording what you have done and tracking its progress. Get into a discussion with other writers and you'd be surprised how many *don't* do this as a matter of course, or at least treat it with casual indifference. It's like planting seeds in the garden but forgetting where you put them and hoping they'll pop up before the slugs get them, to remind you where they are. How would you know not to go over the same ground again two days later?

The main function of keeping a good log is not simply a matter of paper admin. Routine it may be, but it's an important part of the activity. First, it records your output – what *you* have physically produced as a writer – and should include title, word count, file names, etc. Second, it shows where you have sent your work, thus displaying the range of your target market and avoiding the embarrassment of sending the same work twice to the same editor (not a good idea if you want to be taken seriously). Third, reviewing your log on a regular basis will get you into the right frame of mind and motivate you to send out more work or re-write the material that didn't work first time round. Remember: what doesn't press one editor's buttons may well be just what the next one is looking for.

TOP TIPS

- Set yourself deadlines to research and write your current work.

- If not actively writing, at least be thinking about it.

- When nearing completion of one project, start planning the next.

- Keep a log of your submissions for motivation.

You as a Writer (continued)

You can't be a beginner for ever

THERE WILL COME A time when, having written some pieces, maybe sold a few, you might begin to wonder what is the next step in this thing you're doing called being a writer?

Well, one approach is to think about cutting loose – mentally, at least – from the 'beginner' label and start thinking of yourself in a slightly different light.

If, after having completed some projects (whether submitted or not), of entering competitions, of taking writing classes, of slaving over endless manuscripts – or even just a few – you still think of yourself as a beginner, perhaps you need to grasp the nettle and recognise that you are, in fact, a writer.

Imagine for example, finding yourself half a mile out at sea and going down for the third time. A lifeguard comes bobbing along just in time, but in response to your gurgles, he chirps, *Me? I'm just a trainee ...*

There's a hoary old saying often trotted out more in judgemental anger than true wisdom, and usually bellowed with biting self-conviction by an enraged parent, which goes, *Life is not a dress-rehearsal, you know ...!*

Actually, I think life is a whole series, a multitude of dress-rehearsals, where each day is a practice session for the next, each phase of our life a preparation for what lies ahead. The daft thing is, we don't realise it at the time.

In the same way, writing and submitting a story is all practice. Every time. And each work written and submitted, no matter what the outcome, should be treated as a step nearer success. Because whatever else you need in your toolbox to become a published writer, be it ideas, style, voice, stamina or dedication, you need the big-daddy power tool of inner conviction. Without that, you're simply running uphill.

And to grasp that contrived sporting analogy before it slithers between the floorboards and disappears for ever, there are gazillions of runners out there who train daily, weekly or less frequently, for the race they will one day enter. They wear the kit, check the stopwatch, use the correct footwear and clothes and monitor what they eat and drink.

But most of all, they run.

And for a few, training is all they will ever do. Because that's all they need; the self-knowledge that is fed by doing something for the pure, unbridled pleasure of it, not for any tangible adulation or reward.

For others, putting themselves to the ultimate test is a step too far, where the possibility of failure is something they simply cannot contemplate. They may have the talent; they will certainly possess the intent and ability, the sheer will to overcome the many obstacles such as discomfort, lack of time or opportunity – even the call of family or work to do other things instead. But deep down, they still think of themselves as 'training', where shaving off a second or a minute here and there will make all the difference, where just a few more runs will extend their stamina and allow them to compete on terms with the rest of the field. One day.

They may be right. But there's only one true test of ability, and it's the same in writing as it is in sports.

You have to step up to the line.

Instead of thinking of failure, consider how you will deal with success. How will you capitalise on your first (or next) sale? Will you go bigger and better or will you find your niche and enjoy it to the full?

Ask many sports men and women, and they will usually tell you the same thing: coming second is simply not enough. But at least in sports there are three places on the podium to aim for. For writers, there is just one: an acceptance letter.

Equally, ask many keen sports men and women if they constantly try to improve their own times, and the answer will be yes. Shaving off those seconds or minutes is vital, and a reason to celebrate. It may not be a win, but it's a measure of improvement – and a step towards a greater goal.

For most, it's an inner drive which they respond to, something peculiar to each individual. So it is with writers, who see success in many different ways. But most would agree that receiving an acceptance note is a marvellous acknowledgement that they have finally produced something of value which is going to be published for all to see.

We're learning all the time. It's another fascinating aspect of life; that learning never stops. But there's a point at which you have to put that learning to good use, rather than simply doing more of the same. And one way to do that is to think of yourself as a writer. Not merely a beginner.

TOP TIPS

- Don't think of your writing as a step in your training, but as a step towards success.

- Consider your strengths as a writer and use them.

- If you write, you're a writer. The rest is simply a matter of progress.

- Every writer is a beginner at some stage. YOU must decide when you are no longer there.

General Writing Stuff

THERE IS A LOT about being a writer which might come under the general heading of 'None of the Above'. Made up of the bits and pieces, it has probably more to do with the nuts and bolts of the craft rather than anything specific. But it's still there … a bit like the fluff we find in our belly button. It might not be useful, but you never know.

Much of this stuff comes through experience, absorbed through the skin or picked up along the way. I share it with you here, if only because I believe it might help you as it did me.

General Writing Stuff (continued)

What makes a story?

THERE ARE VARIOUS ELEMENTS which go towards making a story, such as a strong descriptive narrative, interesting characters, an unusual setting – even a brooding atmosphere. But, by themselves, they won't necessarily drag the reader beyond the first few words or the opening lines. To do this with any degree of success, and to make sure the reader doesn't lose the will to live and use your story to line the budgie's cage, you need to Make Something Happen.

As an example, I'll paraphrase a certain well-known poem by Felicia Dorothea Hemans.

The boy stood on the deck.

(Yes, I know – a key word is missing … but stick with me.)

As it stands, this is merely a scene – and not a very helpful one. The deck could be on a boat or one of those hardwood patio things; it doesn't tell you about anything else. So what? Well, if we apply the full text of Mrs Hemans' first line, we get a totally different picture:

The boy stood on the <u>burning</u> deck.

Now you have a story – or, at least the beginnings of one. (Especially when the next line tells you that everyone else had bunked off   and not to the pub). The sentence describes the same person and place … but by the addition of a vital word, you have something to sink your teeth into. The word 'burning' spells conflict, danger and the inevitable questions which come rushing at us when the words are used in conjunction. This is what leads us to read on, rather than ignoring it. Questions such as Why? …Who? … and What happens next?

Another example might be to take a seemingly innocuous sentence also describing a person and place:

J stood and marvelled at the beauty of the river.

167

Very nice. But other than allowing the imagination to conjure up a pretty picture of a person looking at a river, there's not much here to draw the reader in. What we need is something to kick the sentence into a whole new dimension.

J stood and marvelled at the beauty of the river, and wondered how cold it would be down on the bottom.

That pretty much takes the 'nice' out of the scene, and should lead even the most incurious of minds to ask why J – whoever she is – should be entertaining such melancholy thoughts. Is she suicidal? Vengeful? Disturbed? Going scuba-diving? Or has she been given a grant by DEFRA to study riverbed temperatures and conditions?

Another sentence, this time describing a common enough street scene, does little to make anyone wonder about whether they should carry on reading

Mac sat in his car at the end of the street.

One might wonder who Mac is and why he's sitting there, but not much more than that. Maybe he's a car stereo nut, or loves the smell of his leather seats and brand-new carpets. By itself, this bland statement won't really tell us. It needs something else.

Mac sat in his car at the end of the street, eyes fixed on the doorway of No 24.

Better – but still not enough. He could be a car nut with a door-knocker fetish.

Mac sat in his car at the end of the street, eyes fixed on the doorway of no 24. His mouth was bone dry, his knuckles white on the wheel ...

Now we're getting somewhere. At the very least, Mac might be about to go and make an offer on a house he can't afford. At worst, he's in need of some anger-management classes. Either way, we're led to imagine all manner of scenarios here ranging from family conflict to a crime or thriller setting.

For a story to begin to work, we need to add in that special element which plucks at the reader's subconscious, be it a word or a supplementary sentence, hinting at something worth delving into but without giving away the whole beeswax. And that element usually involves excitement, danger, threat – or something scratching at our innate curiosity. Almost akin to stepping into the unknown.

In short, we want to know more. And the only way to find out is to continue reading.

But here you have to be careful; part of what makes a story work is not revealing too early what is happening or what is about to happen. Tell everything right at the start, and there's precious little point reading further. No surprise equals no tension.

This drip-feed flow of information, whether in a thriller, romance or any other genre of writing, allows snippets of information to fall on to the page, gradually building a picture for readers to share. Too much, too soon, and there's the danger they might see the ending and give up.

Most stories also need people to make them work. A tree on a hill is merely a tree. Add a person – preferably two – and you have the makings of joy, conflict, a burgeoning relationship or a journey – all the things which make a good read.

TOP TIPS

- Something must happen – or have happened – to make it worthwhile reading on.

- A setting without people is just scenery. It can only last so long before it loses the reader's attention.

- A hint of what lies ahead is enticement enough to draw the reader on.

- Don't reveal too much too soon. Readers have to uncover things for themselves.

General Writing Stuff (continued)

Give yourself a break

IT'S THAT TIME OF year again: the holidays. When people bitten by the writing bug take a long, hard look at the calendar and affirm, 'I'm going to do some serious writing!'

This decision is often accompanied by purchasing a fresh note pad, giving the laptop a wash and brush-up or trying to figure out a way of getting everyone else to push off to Ben Nevis for a few days and leave you in splendidly creative isolation.

Well, sorry to kick sand in your face, but this is remarkably similar to other summer-time promises like, 'I'm going to clear out the loft' ' ...creosote the fence' or ' ...grout the bathroom'. And, like my dear old dad used to say about good intentions, it's all very well trying to put on your wellies while walking downstairs, but you'll probably end up disappointed.

One reason we fail to achieve everything we want to during these all-too-rare breaks is because we set our sights too high. We rarely get all the quiet thinking time we expect or need (yes, staring into space like a hypnotised goldfish is an accepted writerly phenomenon); we find all manner of other distractions for not being able to put words in the order we want to; and instead of being relaxed and ready to let the prose flow from the brain to the paper, we end up stressed, irritable and ready to bite holes in the sun-lounger.

I'm not suggesting, of course, that all your writing plans should be given the elbow just because the rest of the family want you to go to Bognor, Berlin or Barbados. Or because your friends are likely to descend on you like a marauding army the moment you put pen to paper. You probably need the fun just as much as they do anyway.

But what you might do is scale down your expectations

without losing sight of your aims or even being any the less productive.

(Actually, thinking of beaches, I should probably 'fess up straight away and say that I can't recall ever having written anything meaningful on a beach … not unless it was that rude word I carved in the sand at Cromer one summer when I was ten. I think it was only the fact that I mis-spelled it that saved my bacon.)

I've scribbled to good effect on trains, yes; boats, too – and planes – especially when I've wanted to avoid conversation. Even walks in the country have produced that blinding 'Yes!' moment, when a problem was overcome with a flash of inspiration. But never by the sea. Too much sand in delicate places, too much weather, too much nature and way too much going on around me to be ignored. Although, on the last point, I once sat on a deserted Cape Cod beach and got endless enjoyment watching absolutely nothing go by. It was brilliant!

So, the thing to do is set your aims to suit the circumstances. Instead of trying to write a short story in its entirety, why not simply sketch out the main characters and an outline plot – maybe even two? For a planned feature, jot down a tick-list of the points you want to cover – maybe even the illustrations or photos you could use to go with it. For something more ambitious (yes, the book) rough out what you would like to see happen as main events in the plot. List the characters, with whatever descriptive details might occur to you, and the locations. Even build some idea of the chapters and their contents to suit the flow of the story.

Vague as it may seem, what you are doing is working on building a framework which, by its very looseness, will give you a number of useful options about what to do next.

You're not being bogged down at this point by unnecessary detail or structure, nor are you lured into going over the same points again and again due to fractured concentration. And none of these scribblings needs to be hugely accurate or in any specific order; all that can come later. It's merely another use of the stepping stone process I've mentioned before, but it can lead to real progress.

So much better, I find, than staring in bug-eyed frustration at a blank screen or note pad and wondering whether, if you buried the noisy g*t next door in the nearest flower bed (along with his strimmer), would anyone notice?

I find this shorthand form of creativity much easier – and in the end, considerably more satisfying than trying to write against all odds. In fact, it's as though the very act of *not* trying too hard unleashes a buzz of ideas. And being able to refer back to my 'notes' at any time, no matter how unstructured they might be, allows me more flexibility in what I'm doing.

It also lets me face that first holiday gin and tonic of the day with a real feeling of accomplishment. And accomplishment, to most of us, is surely what it's all about.

TOP TIPS

- Don't set unrealistic writing aims when you know circumstances are not in your favour.

- Random jottings can be just as productive as a full page.

- Prepare a framework, then fill in the detail when time allows.

- A relaxed mind is far more creative than a stressed one.

- Don't forget, have some fun, too.

General Writing Stuff (continued)

Picture the scene ...

DESCRIBING SCENERY IS JUST one element of writing a story, along with plot, characters and action. It provides the reader with backdrop and atmosphere, and with all of us being able to travel almost anywhere these days, a recognisable landscape where we may feel a sense of *déjà vu*. For example, go to New York, Paris, London or any big city, and you might feel that you've been there before. If you haven't, you've probably read about it or seen it on-screen.

Depending on how you handle the description of scenery, it can be a vital part of your writing. It can influence the way a reader pictures a scene, and can add to the tension of a particular piece. But, if too detailed, it can get in the way of what you are trying to convey.

When we describe a street scene, we are often calling up an image of somewhere we may have seen before – a fragment from experience. What we remember will differ from the real place to one degree or another, because that's the way the memory plays tricks with us. If there's a gap, the brain automatically fills it in with something else. But unless we're trying to describe a real place in vivid detail, that's not so important; what is, is the general image, as a backdrop for the action we're describing.

A useful way of honing our 'view' of scenery, is to practise it. And a good place to start is right outside where we live. You'll have seen the area around your home thousands of times, under different conditions. That includes weather, light, time of day or night – even your own frame of mind, depending on mood, company, situation or level of intoxication (I jest, of course). Thus, if you were to write down what lies right outside your own front door, it would depend largely on how you last saw it.

A useful exercise (which has two parts) is to step outside and look at what you can see. I mean *really* study it, noting everything as though it were for the first time: buildings, people, trees, street furniture, vehicles, weather conditions, light – everything. Then step back inside, and, without looking back, write down a description of the scene outside *as if* you were writing it into a story or novel. If it helps, picture it through the eyes of your current main character, and use the language he or she would employ to describe it. Don't forget, sounds are important, too. How about the drone of a plane, the buzz of a tractor or the sound of children – all of which may be transitory, but which can add significantly to atmosphere and a feeling for the kind of place it is?

Now print it out and read it. Then go back outside and compare the two. You will have probably missed some things completely, even moved one or two without realising it. You may even have placed something in the scene which isn't there at all.

The interesting thing is that, if you were to go through this exercise with a friend or two, you would find that the difference in what was seen, against what was written down, even by two or more people on the same spot at the same time, would be considerably different. It's all down to memory and perception.

(I once conducted this exercise with a writers' group in a school building, and while some described a lengthy row of rubbish skips in the playground immediately below, others missed them altogether and focussed on objects on the other side of the school premises. It was only when they went back to the window that they each realised how much they had missed.)

The second part of the exercise is to edit what the eye has seen. With all the points you may have included in your description, if you tried to put them in a story, you'd end up with pages of detail that nobody would want to read. A rambling list of every item that might be out there is not necessary and will detract from the tension, quite apart from being pretty boring. A street lamp is only of interest if referred to in a night scene; a bush is only sinister if there's a chance that someone is hiding behind it; and a picturesque garden is only noteworthy if being referred to as a backdrop to characters standing in it.

What you have to do is distil what you have seen outside your door to a few lines, while still managing to convey something recognisable. More than that, you should try to convey a sense of atmosphere, either by referring to light, movement, noise, shadow or shapes – all in a few words without slinging in the whole scene, down to the flea-bitten dog wandering past on the other side.

Some writers manage to convey description and atmosphere in a single sentence; others take a bit more. But what all the good ones do is show the scene, then get on with the action.

TOP TIPS

- Practise taking mental snaps-shots and writing them down.

- Look for items which add to atmosphere or the appearance of a place.

- Write down what you see, then edit it down to the bare minimum.

- Don't forget sounds, which can be very atmospheric.

Reviewing your writing tools

LIKE ANYONE ELSE IN the creative business, writers need certain tools to do their job. Whether using pen and paper or computer, without them we would find it difficult to do what we do – which is putting down words on paper for others to read. It is no different to a bricklayer needing a trowel, spirit level and mortar; they are fundamental requirements.

But just as a bricklayer needs the basics, he also needs plans, materials and somewhere to build. And writers should also consider the intangibles which are vital to the creative process.

Ask writers what they value most, and you're likely to get a variety of answers ranging from peace and quiet through to simply having plenty of fresh ideas on tap. (Add to that the latest piece of electronic hardware or software, since we are, like it or not, bedded into the age where some think a good computer will make us better writers. It won't, but it will help the process.)

Let us examine atmosphere as a tool. A friend of mine works at her kitchen table. She does so because she feels it is her 'place' and she can sit down whenever the mood takes her. She also worries that friends will think she's putting on airs if she bags a specific room to do her writing. Unfortunately, what is her place to write is also a major trade route for the rest of creation; family, pets, children from down the street, neighbours and visiting family members, all wanting a slice of her time. No wonder she complains of not getting enough peace to write.

Another friend tucks himself away in the spare room where nobody can get at him. Up there, he plays classical music and gets in the mood. Well, almost. Unfortunately, he often finds he can't get in the 'right' mood for the words to flow, and ends up wandering the house like a refugee, trying to find where he left it.

Atmosphere is important, and varies according to the individual. Friend A needs to allocate herself a specific place where she can work in comfort with the minimum of interruption. Friend B needs to think about how, in the kind of place A can only dream of, he needs to create the right ambiance.

In both cases, they are victims of their own circumstances. Having a quiet place to write is not a crime, not is it pretentious, silly or even suspect. We wouldn't, after all, expect a keen gardener to be satisfied using a tub in the middle of the living room carpet.

Friend A, if her writing is that important to her, needs to grasp the nettle and inform the family that she needs somewhere for herself. She isn't locking herself away like a hermit crab, merely distancing herself for a while from the hurly-burly.

Friend B needs to think about what he is writing, and how the music he plays fits into that. Classical music may be something he enjoys, but it might be wrong for his frame of mind while writing. He could try varying the output to alter his mood. A gentle violin piece may be too bland for creating a suspense story, and a piece of Wagner rattling the rafters certainly won't do much for a story of soft candlelight and whispered sweet nothings.

Or how about some actual peace and quiet? Now there's a thing.

Another tool we tend to forget is a good source of reference. How often do we *know* the kind of word we need, yet can't quite bring it to mind? How accurate is our geography in a story – details of which might be subsequently picked apart by an editor at the expense of all our hard work? How often do we forget that what we knew even five years ago has changed dramatically because of shifting circumstances? (I must confess to this mistake once, when I quoted a 40-minute journey time from one part of London to another – a trip I used to take regularly. An editor queried whether I had done so recently, since that time has now doubled as a result of increased traffic, the congestion zone and reduced speed limits, which impacted quite seriously on the flow and time-plan of my story.)

Thinking time is another tool we tend to overlook. Taking time out to think seriously about where our story is going can pay real dividends, rather than just giving it the odd thought over dinner along with interest rates, the children's schooling and that bald tyre on the car.

Thinking, allied with jotting down ideas, alternative plots, 'what ifs' and some wild mind-mapping on scrap paper, can often serve to unblock the creative processes far more effectively than labouring painfully over a hot keyboard. So can walking, window-shopping or performing some other automatic task.

Our tools are important for us to do the job, whether it is part- or full-time. Having the right ones at hand – and reviewing them from time to time – could make all the difference between a job done well or simply snatched at and wasted.

TOP TIPS

- Think about atmosphere and place. Are yours suitable for writing?

- Take your writing time seriously and others will do so, too.

- Having sources of reference at hand will save time and effort.

- Give yourself time to think about what you are doing and where you are going.

Don't run out of puff

IT'S AMAZING WHAT A difference a couple of decades makes. In a second-hand bookshop recently, I found a couple of novels I hadn't seen in nearly thirty years. One of the first things that struck me (apart from the wonderful, musty smell – try getting that out of an electronic reader) was how breathless I became while reading. No, it was nothing to do with decades of dust invading my respiratory tract. What I found was that most of the sentences seemed to run on for line after line, broken only by the occasional comma, until I began looking for the full stop rather than enjoying the story. Mentally, at least, I was rather like a sprinter, lunging for the finish line before running out of puff, or a driver going faster to reach a service area before running out of petrol. (You've never done that? Sheesh, you haven't lived.)

This type of extended sentence was clearly something I hadn't really noticed first time round, most likely because the style of much writing years ago was for longer, all-embracing passages, with a few asides along the way to impart important ancillary information and additional comments thrown in as the writer felt fit, to give colour, depth and background, like this one, dear and no doubt by now, equally breathless reader. (See what I mean?)

Since then, thank goodness, there has been something of a change. How this came about, I'm not sure. But most fiction now goes for a shorter, punchier style of sentence, perhaps suiting modern communication means and speech patterns.

This discovery coincided with me being on a panel of judges for a short-fiction competition. The theme was open, so the entrants were varied. Many had adopted the current style, using shorter sentences sprinkled with current expressions and references, or the odd throwaway comment by the narrator. But a few used a more literary style, with florid language and longer sentences.

This seemed to work well when the subject matter or setting was of a historical or 'serious' nature. However, I found myself having to re-read a couple with a more contemporary setting, because it seemed to jar a little. It wasn't simply that the words used seemed out of context, or that the flowery description sometimes got in the way of the basic story; it was that the sentences seemed longer than I was used to, and littered with extraneous bits of information like sheep's wool on a barbed-wire fence. With some, this merely spoiled the tension of the storytelling, killing what might have been an interesting or captivating passage. Had it been a book, it would have been less noticeable, given the greater space available for expansion of a theme or descriptive narrative. But in a short story, where getting to the point is paramount, it was all too visible.

Equally, I suppose, telling a story with a period setting, but using modern colloquialisms – *Why,' pon my soul, Mr Darcy, innit* – would be just as jarring. (Unless it were a deliberate parody, of course. Sadly, there were none of these, which might have been fun, and likely to have carried away a prize for originality.)

A series of shorter sentences with full stops is quite useful if you wish to convey tension. Where describing a dynamic action scene, for example, you might need to make the style punchier, to reflect the kind of event being portrayed.

This is also useful in a more reflective piece where you may have a first-person narrator under some emotional, physical or mental strain, and you wish to convey this as if his or her thoughts and conclusions are being ripped out of them in a series of sharp, painful tugs, rather than as if it were a carefully worded discussion over a pleasant glass of sherry and one elbow on the mantelpiece. (And if anyone out there below a certain age wants to know what the heck a mantelpiece is, you either live in a modern house or you need to read some older books – they're peppered with them.)

Dialogue is another example where shorter can be better.

Most people speak in short bursts, interspersed with pauses, 'umms' and 'ahs' rather than long, fluent speech. I'm not suggesting you include all these exclamations in your writing, because that would be intensely irritating and might lead to severe book abuse. But using brevity in an exchange of dialogue is certainly more true-to-life, and allows you to move the action along while giving a sense of the often rapid ebb and flow of characters' intentions and reactions as they speak.

This is particularly evident where an argument is raging. Most writers instinctively allow each character to take their turn, whereas in real life, there are interruptions, pauses and overlapping speech. Again, to include all this in a passage would be detrimental, but the occasional interruption or flare-up would show verisimilitude and allow movement down the page in a series of shorter, sharper sentences with, perhaps, movement and action to break up the speech.

TOP TIPS

- Match the style of language and delivery to the setting.

- Reflect tension by the use of punchier sentences.

- Would two short sentences be more effective than one long one?

- Be wary of monologues – alternate dialogue is more interesting to read.

General Writing Stuff (continued)

Work in progress

IT'S TEMPTING TO THINK that these three words should be on a notice pinned to your door in big, bold letters so that your nearest and dearest can see when you DON'T want to walk the dog, collect the kids from school, paint the Sistine Chapel or run a couple of marathons backwards with a candelabra balanced on your head.

However, work in progress (or WIP as it's known in the manufacturing industry) is something all writers are involved in, consciously or otherwise, all the time.

Like most scribes, I have an 'Ideas' folder, where I place all my back-of-the-envelope scribblings until they're needed. These can range from thoughts about follow-on books in a series, to vague jottings about characters, names, plots or scenes which I might use in the future. Whatever they are – and this is largely psychological, I admit – I prefer to think of them as works in progress, no matter how vague or unformed they might appear at the time – especially to an outsider. (And boy, looking at one just recently, if the notes had fallen into the hands of a zealous policeman, I'd have probably been introduced to some rubber hose treatment, such was the wording: *kill street youth – body of woman – bogus church group – kidnap teenager – blackmail parents.)*

Not, as one might think, the ravings of a would-be psychopath planning his next evening out, but a working writer's ideas being jotted down for later use (and which, incidentally, became my third book).

And this is how most writing begins: as a seemingly random collection of words, on the way to becoming something more concrete. But for it to become that, the ideas have to be continually reviewed to see if anything sparks off into a workable story, otherwise they shrivel and die.

A way of not letting such valuable thoughts moulder is to immediately add a few words, allowing your instincts to kick in, and sketching out how you think the idea might grow and which direction it could take. Thus, in the heat of the moment, use that flash of inspiration, garnered through seeing something, hearing a snatch of conversation, reading a headline or whatever, and take it one stage further by jotting down a few extra words to make it more than just a passing thought. This way, you're setting up a chain of ideas for the future, even if you change it completely later.

In the case above, I'd been reading about the death of a rough sleeper in London's West End, and started thinking about what might have caused it *other* than drugs, disease or malnutrition (it's always worth trying to find an alternative to the obvious, if only to make you think harder about something fresher and less tried).

At the time, there had also been a story running in the US about a bogus church charity preying on vulnerable runaways, and this gave me the idea of marrying the two events and combining them into a single story. The rest fell into place bit by bit.

Of course, my initial idea might have easily fallen by the wayside or become something else entirely. But by thinking of it as a work in progress, I was committing myself to looking at it seriously and trying to build it into something solid.

The important thing is to never let a good idea go to waste.

My WIP folder contains all manner of oddments like this, and I regularly trawl through them to see if anything gives me that spark which will set me off on to a new project. It may be a short story, it could be an idea for a novel. But whatever it is destined to be, I see that WIP folder as being full of workable nuggets which I will get round to one day. And whenever I dip into it, I usually find myself adding a thought or two to one of the documents, like bricks in a wall, until one begins to take on an energy of its own. Eventually, that document will 'go critical' until I can't leave it alone any longer and it becomes a tangible piece of work with a deadline or a market in mind.

Occasionally, one of these ideas may be used subconsciously elsewhere, either in total or cannibalised to fit another work. It's therefore essential to cull them on a regular basis and leave only the fresher ones to work on.

The other aspect of my WIP folder is that anything in it stays there until it's completed *and submitted*. Only then do I transfer it into a different folder for finished work which is out in the market place. Why? Because by definition, anything in the WIP folder is still being worked on, polished, buffed up, amended – all those things we writers do until we're satisfied we've done a good job and can send it to an editor with a clear conscience.

TOP TIPS

- Ideas need fleshing out, without which they remain undeveloped.

- Review your WIP folder on a regular basis and weed out any dead wood or add thoughts to others where you can.

- A WIP folder means you are never in the position of not having something to work on.

- A work in progress is merely that until it's submitted or sold.

- Your WIP folder is your breeding ground for the future.

General Writing Stuff (continued)

It's called make-believe

NEVER ONE TO PASS up on a good quote when I see one, I read recently in the Saturday *Times* supplement, columnist Robert Crampton describing how conversations between him and his young son consist of ...*taking two worlds that* do *exist and smashing them together to make one that doesn't.*

My immediate thought was, what an appropriate way to describe writing fiction. As writers, we're accustomed to using things that we know of in the real world and bringing them together to make another world which doesn't exist. (Except in our heads, of course, where anything is possible and obscenely big book deals *do* happen.)

One might argue that since everything we've used in our fictional scenarios has been copied to one degree or another from real life, then it *is* real. Well, not quite. Because we're merely borrowing those things (scenes, characters, items, events) and slotting them into a world which only *resembles* the one we know, but is entirely false.

Of course, certain pseuds might argue that, look, dude, y'know, existentially speaking, what you've created is just, well, a *construct*, see, fashioned from reality, so in effect, it must be, well ... real, right?

No.

It's made up!

Characters. We might dare, bearing in mind the ever-increasing litigious nature of those around us, 'borrow' certain facets of people we know, to help us give flesh to our fictional heroes and villains. Even characters in sci-fi or fantasy books will bear certain similarities to real people. But the personae we create are still not going to be real. They may seem like someone we know by appearance, sound or manner; they may even have a similar name – although I'd advise against that, personally, it's pushing your luck a bit. They may even be based on fictional characters created by someone else. But they will only ever be what we have created in our minds. (Incidentally, just in case a certain someone down the street is wondering, the miserable old biddy in a blue hat described in my last book was pure coincidence).

Events. Many stories and books borrow from true events in history, to give weight or realism to the plot, or to attract a certain type of reader. Some may even be written as reconstructions of true events, but with a strong fictional twist. But whatever a work might borrow in this way, some of the original elements will eventually be taken in another direction entirely according to the whims and requirements of the author, because that's what writing fiction is all about. We take what we know (or know about) and amend it where necessary in order to make it fit our scheme of things.

Items. Again, making allowances for specific genres, the majority of things we describe, be they cars, houses, clothes, guns or teapots, are familiar to us because it's far easier to write about something you can see or touch than something you cannot. It helps if they also have some familiarity to the reader. An object which they have read about, used or seen before, brings instant recognition without the constant mental question mark popping up over something they've never heard of. Once or twice in a book might be acceptable, especially where someone is venturing into a genre they haven't tried before, but too many of these and it becomes like a technical manual and the reader will begin to lose track and interest.

Scenery. There's a healthy divide on this point, but, like many authors, I prefer to use real places in my books, rather than invented ones. The main reason is laziness; real places are easier to write about and describe (even if I transpose them somewhere else entirely). However, if I do need to get a named location spot-on accurate, I can visit the place and do the necessary research. It's worth bearing in mind that readers love to spot places that are familiar to them, too, and if that helps bring them back to your books, then all to the good.

That doesn't mean you shouldn't be able to alter certain aspects of a place if it happens to suit your storyline. And that's the great thing about making it all up; it may be based on a real place, but it will never *be* entirely real. Put in a pub? Easy job. Straighten a road for an action scene? Couldn't be simpler. Drop in a nightclub where there isn't one? Consider it done, my son. Some left-over tarmac? Oh, hang on ...

Outcomes. This is where the head really flies off the hammer, as my dear old dad used to say. (I never knew what it meant, either – I'm just borrowing ...) Anyway, the outcome of our story is when whatever else we may have borrowed from the real world, be it people, places, guns, cars, houses or rainstorms, becomes less than real. It has to, because what becomes of our heroes and villains is pure fiction. Most of us, after all, don't consciously write an ending to a story which is true in real life. Where's the fun in that? If, after having dragged our loyal and wonderfully generous readers on a journey which we've, y'know, dude, *made up* from elements of real life, the very least we can do is give them a larger than life, different to life and much more thrilling than life ending. That way, they might just come back for more.

It's called make-believe.

TOP TIPS

- In fiction, you can use real objects, places or events for inspiration – but the finished work is still make-believe.

- Using real events as a backdrop or starting point can lead to a new dramatic 'take' on history.

- Using real people can help colour your characters – but be careful of going too far.

- It's your fiction, your world; you can do anything you like.

General Writing Stuff (continued)

Don't throw out your babies

THERE COMES A MOMENT when most writers want to 'see rubbish as far as it will go' as my dear old granny used to say. Or in writerly terms, rip up something that doesn't seem to be working and hurl it at the nearest waste bin.

And very therapeutic it can be, too, after slaving on a piece which simply won't roll over and do what you want it to. (It's probably a boy thing, but I find it especially satisfying when I can slam-dunk a manuscript from across the room without having to get up and retrieve the scattered pages from all over the furniture. Well, we writers have to take our pleasures where we can find them.)

However, dumping a print-out is one thing; with a PC, you can always go back after you've thought it over and retrieve the file. Killing off a piece of work altogether – deleting the file – is something else. It's like burning your only paper copy; it's final. Irreversible. Gone for good. (Unless you're a techno-nut and can rummage about in the guts of your PC without causing meltdown – which most of us are not).

I made the mistake of throwing away any number of ideas when I started out as a writer, simply because I thought they were useless. When something wasn't going right, I'd simply dump the whole idea and start again. Fresh paper, fresh plots … my brain was full to bursting with them, so why not?

Yet, as I found out recently when I happened on a diskette containing some stuff I had never submitted for publication, there's potential gold in them thar electronic hills, given a bit of a tweak here and there. Perhaps distance has lent my earlier scribblings an imagined freshness (to me, anyway), but in going over one or two of them, I found they weren't all that bad.

True, the terminology could do with some revamping; in one

I mentioned the 'forthcoming' channel tunnel. And there was no mention of mobile phones – this was written only a few years ago, I hasten to add – which can change the whole course and make-up of a story. But while some of the settings could do with being more appealing, rather than the gritty places I used to write about, some of the basic ideas have travelled surprisingly well over the years.

And here is an important point: quite simply, tastes change over time, and good editors tune into this. Witness the renewed interest in historical novels recently, and the explosion of readers looking for the next fantasy novel. Just a short time ago, bookshop shelves devoted to these genres were fairly small, which must have led many writers to concentrate on something judged more 'commercial'. Yet how many of them could benefit now by hauling out their old manuscripts and giving them a literary facelift?

If we look at what we wrote even just a couple of years ago, which was either confined to a remote computer file or the bottom drawer of a desk somewhere because it didn't seem suitable, we may find elements in there which can be rescued and even resuscitated – re-marketed – as something different.

Depending on how long ago they first saw the light of day, bringing the story up to date would be the first job to tackle. There's nothing like outmoded language – especially slang – to date a story; and there's much in the detail which can change the whole feel of a piece quite easily. Merely mentioning mobile phones or text messaging is one way, or dropping in the title of a film, a song or a make of car, any of which can give a story a more current feel. Maybe revamping the slant of the story, while retaining the original idea which got you started in the first place, is a way of bringing it out and making it more saleable.

The point of view is another approach. What may have sounded stilted and unconvincing in the third person (he said/ she said) might take on a whole new freshness when told from a first person viewpoint. Telling the story through the eyes of the central character makes you consider the detail of the story completely differently; you have only the single view to worry about, and there's an intimacy when bringing in the thought processes of that character which the third person viewpoint may have prevented you exploring.

Another reason to review your 'backlist' of unsold or previously never-submitted work is simply to give yourself a break. Any one of us can get tired and stale without really noticing. This usually hits home when you find you've been staring at the PC for more minutes than is good for you, yet you have nothing concrete on the screen to show for it. Effectively, you can end up going round in circles.

Instead, why not take a gentle stroll back through those old files, or dig out that bunch of manuscripts you could never quite bring yourself to get rid of. And if you're one of those writers who habitually chucks work away when it doesn't seem to work, try hanging on to it. You never know – one day it might surprise you.

TOP TIPS

- Never throw anything away – you might be able to re-write or cannibalise it later.

- Regularly review your old scripts for useable scenes.

- Bring old or unused stories or ideas up-to-date by introducing current language and descriptions.

- Try re-writing a story from another point-of-view. It could work wonders.

Fate accompli

THERE'S AN OLD GAG about a driver who stops to ask an old man for directions. After a few moments of careful thought, the old man says, 'Well, first off, I wouldn't start from *here* … '

Joking apart, the same thought can be applied to writing: effectively, are we starting from the correct point in our story, or approaching from the right angle? There is always another way of looking at a scene, and the one you first think of might not be the best. This applies whether we're at the start of the story or beginning a fresh chapter or scene, say, in a novel.

As an example, I once had in mind a particular opening scene for a story. It hinged on a murder, where the victim had heavy chains tied to his feet and was lowered into an indoor swimming pool to die. It was a fairly dark scene and I'm still not sure where it sprang from, only that, once in the story-grinder, it had to come out.

To gain a feel for the atmosphere, I visited our local pool when it was quiet, to get a sense of a deserted poolside (the murder was committed at night). I also wanted to capture the floor texture, smells, damp air, sounds, echoes and so forth. OK, I stopped short of actually hurling myself into the pool with a hundredweight of ships' bling round my ankles, but there are limits to the lengths of my research.

It was while writing up my notes that I had a thought: what if, instead of beginning with the scene of the murder, which was by its nature fairly brutal, I went for another angle? After all, describing violence might be attention-grabbing, but where did it leave me afterwards? And did it help the story?

The result was, I scrapped my original scene and opened the story later that day. This time, with the central character – an amateur sleuth – looking down at the dead man standing on the bottom of the pool, his body moving gently in the water. Nearby floated a curled strip of soggy cardboard.

Effectively, this after-the-event opening allowed me to skip the violence (which didn't really advance the story) and stopped me revealing too much detail about the – pardon the pun – execution. That, after all, was what I wanted my sleuth to find out, since that's what sleuths are for.

It still gave me ample room for atmosphere, tension and the horror of finding someone killed in this way. And rather than describing how the killing was done, I left it to my sleuth to notice how the dead man was clutching the lane marker rope, which he'd tried to use to pull himself out and was keeping his body upright. He also worked out later the horrible significance of the strip of soggy cardboard. (The killers had prolonged the victim's agony by handing him a cardboard tube from a kitchen foil roll to breathe through. Being cardboard …well, you get the idea …)

Switching the order of approach like this is quite useful. Instead of going through events as they actually happen, which can sometimes be too revealing, you can bring them on almost in flashback, interspersing them with your central character's thoughts, suspicions or fears. This is particularly useful for crime stories, where you want the reader to follow up the clues as well, thereby increasing the tension. But it can work just as well in other genres, where a character might be reviewing, say, family events loaded with emotion and meaning, rather like a slide-show, and drawing conclusions from it which may have a life-shattering effect on others.

The post-event opening can work in other powerful ways. Describing a car accident can be difficult to pull off without making it sound cartoon-ish. But opening the scene *after* the accident, describing the driver coming to, the tick-tick of a spinning wheel, the silence, the smell of fuel and the horrifying drip of liquid – can be much more shocking. This is because the reader's mind is automatically filling in the gaps, creating a vivid picture of his own making.

Changing the point at which we describe a scene can also work if we change the viewpoint – in other words, who sees what. Having a character walk unexpectedly into a meeting, for example, can be full of tension seen from that character's viewpoint – particularly in the reading of a will. Imagine viewing it from *inside* the room, describing perhaps a self-satisfied and expectant bunch of graspers, all of whom think they've got it settled. Then in comes the unwelcome interloper. This could bring out a whole raft of additional tensions and reactions, so that rather than seeing the reaction through one pair of eyes, we're seeing it through many.

A simple test is to take the last scene you worked on and start from a different angle. It will undoubtedly make you write the scene in a different way, but it might also give you thoughts about future projects.

TOP TIPS

- Describing events as they unfold can sometimes 'reveal' more than you want.

- Coming in on a scene *after* an event can improve tension and give direction for future narrative.

- Change the viewpoint, change the drama.

- The silence *after* a crash can be more dramatic than the crash itself.

- Allow the reader to fill in some of the gaps.

Time for a spring-clean

MY DEAR OLD MOTHER used to announce on a regular basis that it was the time of year for a good spring-clean. It wasn't always spring, but she used the occasion to go from basement to loft, chucking out anything that was no longer useful and refurbishing that which had a grain of promise left in it.

Which, for writers, is no bad habit to get into occasionally, whatever the season. Most of us, if honest, are usually so focussed on our current project that we tend not to see the rubbish accumulating around us. Yet this rubbish can either prevent us getting on with something new, or might even contain a hint of promise. But we won't know until we look.

Submissions. Firstly, check the back catalogue of work. Assuming they were actually sent off, did you ever receive a reply to all your submissions? If longer than three months, a polite letter to the editor(s) wouldn't go amiss, suggesting that while going through your records, you'd noticed that no response had been received and wondered if ...? Many a story or feature has lain dormant in somebody's in-tray until retrieved this way, and if you don't chase it, it's a sure thing nobody else will.

Sales/successes. Have you recorded your successes? If paid, you need to account for any income received, and you should keep a record of any expenses. Both of these elements are required for tax purposes, even if you are not a full-time writer.

Even if your work is unpaid, you should always keep a record of the magazines you submit to, thus avoiding the embarrassment of sending the same piece to the same editor twice.

Bottom drawer. Whether you keep a hoard of mouldering, unsold manuscripts in a drawer or have the equivalent stored on electronic media, you should go through them every now and then to see whether any are still useful or should be given the deep six with a trumpet voluntary at the bottom of the garden.

My own practice is never to throw anything away, but then I'm an eternal optimist. I also hoard old nails, screws, bolts and washers in a tin box, and countless lengths of wood with no earthly use beyond a roaring good bonfire. On the other hand, you never know – they may come in handy one day.

That said, even I have been forced to concede on occasion that something I have laboured over long into the night, then left quietly gestating in the hopes that it would spring into something magnificent, is a bit of a damp squib, with about as much chance of springing anywhere as a concrete cess-pit. The kindest fate is to take a deep breath and confine it to oblivion, thus putting us both out of its misery.

The other reason for cleaning out the old files is that shedding some light on dusty corners sometimes breathes life where it was thought there might be none left. Reading over old stories can either bring inspiration for other ideas or, at best, make you realise that what you wrote in the past actually wasn't all that bad.

Tools for the job. More of a review than a clean, but are you using the best equipment for the job? Isn't it time you traded in that lumpy old PC for a newer model, or changed that beloved, but temperamental printer for something a little more sprightly and obedient? And how about your reference books? Are they a bit long in the tooth – especially for current idiom and terminology? And your filing system? Still using an old shoebox held together by sticky tape and stuffed into the back of the wardrobe, or might you be better served by being a little more professional and organised?

Presentation. On the professional tack, is your presentation as good as it might be? Do you have a decent letterhead, compliment slips and invoices, which are basic requirements for a writer, and simple to produce on a decent printer? A neat and professional-looking presentation can dramatically affect how you appear to editors and even how you view yourself. In the same way, paper and envelopes don't need to be costly, but a manuscript produced on decent (at least 80gram) white paper and submitted in an A4 size envelope will look good. And even if it comes back with a refusal, it stands a better chance of being used again.

Direction. Even our ideas and plans can stand an occasional brush-up. And spring is a good time to review where we're going as a writer. Fiction or features – or both? Strictly short work or is it time to try something lengthier? If you've had absolutely no luck with one particular genre of writing compared with others, it could be time to concentrate on where you are successful, and focus on your strengths.

Goals. Finally, and perhaps most important, have you been putting off completing something – or worse, beginning? If you are one of those who regularly says 'I'll do it when I get time.' then why not make the time and use it as a springboard (excuse the pun) to throw yourself whole-heartedly into doing what you have endlessly promised yourself. Put aside fears, ignore the pitfalls, lapses and – dare I say it – doubting friends or family, and make *today* the beginning of something new.

TOP TIPS

- Check your work records are up to date on submissions, sales and accounts.

- Look at returned stories to see if they can be recycled.

- Check out old story ideas to see if time and distance has given you a fresh perspective on them.

- Make sure you are using the best writing tools for the job.

- Take a fresh look at markets and guidelines, to see if you are up-to-date on current requirements.

General Writing Stuff (continued)

Let your writing cook

A FEMALE FAMILY MEMBER who shall remain nameless announced recently that she had read all the right cook books, from Mrs Beaton to the latest Jamie Oliver, and watched all manner of cookery programmes, but had never really thought of herself as a good cook. (A view, incidentally, shared and endorsed by the rest of the family – but that's a whole other story.) However, it was a revealing comment which set me thinking.

While I'm undoubtedly not the first person to have made the connection, it occurred to me that cooking and writing are not so very different. Both are creative; both require the following of certain rules or recipes and, depending on the mix or ingredients, both can end up as a satisfying meal ... or a complete dog's dinner (darn – another cliché). In addition, both depend on varying carefully the degrees of heat, activity and colour to complete the finished product.

Declaring my credentials from the outset, I have been known to slave away over both keyboard and cooker with equal enthusiasm. It's also true to say I have met with equal diversity of success in both activities.

My problem with cooking is that I rarely follow a recipe beyond the name of the dish. Call it boredom (I prefer to call it creative curiosity) but before I'm halfway down the list of ingredients, I'm scouring the cupboard for something a little different; that extra spice that might add a certain zest to the mix. The fact that I occasionally find the wrong one can sometimes be discovered in the dog, but the end result is usually agreeable ... and I haven't poisoned anyone yet.

With writing, the cooking instructions are the equivalent to the do's and don'ts mentioned here and elsewhere – the framework on which one builds the story. The main ingredient is what tells readers the genre of story they are reading, be it romance, thriller, fantasy and so forth; the fish, if you like, to fish pie. You can use meat instead, but while you might still end up with something very enjoyable, it definitely won't be fish pie.

While sticking with the main ingredient is important if you wish to keep to a particular genre, there's nothing wrong with looking for ways to spice up the flow of the narrative from time to time. And in the same way that not every dot and comma of a recipe needs to be adhered to, you shouldn't shy away from lobbing the occasional surprise into your writing, too.

This might take the form of introducing a fresh, surprising character or event, either of which can cause a shift in the pace and direction of your story if done in the right way. It could be the setting or time frame, where instead of a story stretched over a day or several days, it could be one confined to a couple of hours or even a few minutes. This might have the effect of making you focus on specific details which you might not do as a normal rule.

Try sprinkling in a bit more emotion; drop in more tension; stir in a soupcon of occasional humour between your characters, and let the whole shebang bubble away.

After a suitable gap, go back and see what it tastes like. You might be surprised.

Another comparison with the culinary arts is that there will come a point at which the story really begins to 'cook'; when having brought together all the various components, beaten, chopped, cut and diced, things begin to simmer nicely. This is an almost organic process, where your characters take on a life of their own, or the story begins to suggest its own direction without enormous effort from you.

Naturally, this is also the point where you have to exercise a little control over the flame, otherwise you might end up overcooking things.

One specific warning: if you are writing for a particular market, rather than as an exercise, don't ignore the market guidelines. Experimenting with your writing is fine, as long as you don't wander off into the wilder realms and make the story unsuitable. No matter how cleverly you assemble the concoction, whether writing or cooking, if you don't pay sufficient attention to what your consumer wants, you may end up with an unhappy punter (ie: the editor or reader).

As proved by my Auntie Jean (damn – I've gone and outed her), you can read as many books on a subject as you like. But while they will help you along the way and provide lots of useful tips and guidelines, following them slavishly won't automatically guarantee success.

The truth is that there are times when it's worth flinging away the recipe book and going for broke, to ignore what you've done before and try something a little different.

To use another analogy – that of a child on its first bicycle – you never know what you can do until you kick away the stabilisers and launch yourself into the unknown. Yes, you may wobble; you may even take a tumble or two. But, unlike falling off a bike, you won't hurt yourself. What you might do is discover something in your writing that you never knew you possessed. You might also gain a sense of freedom and a huge feeling of fun and achievement – and that's what writing should be all about.

TOP TIPS

- Follow the recipe (the guidelines and the usual format of the book or story).

- Be brave and try 'cooking' something different every now and then. You never know what you can do until you try.

- If the finished product seems lacking in excitement, spice it up a little with some action, a new character or a sudden plot turn.

- The 'meal' has to please you first. If so, it stands a better chance of pleasing others.

General Writing Stuff (continued)

Writing to win

SOMEWHERE BACK IN THE dim mists of time, a businessman once remarked, 'There's nothing like a bit of competition'. You can bet your boots he was probably the market leader. Either that or he wasn't as noble as he pretended and was planning to fire-bomb his nearest competitor while nobody was looking.

Luckily, writers are (mostly) a gentler, more generous sector of the community and there's nothing like a bit of competition – more precisely, a writing competition – to get one's creative juices flowing. Furthermore, with some of the substantial prizes on offer, they can also generate some welcome revenue.

A gazillion words have been written on this subject, but it doesn't hurt to look at the competition process from the same viewpoint from which you should be approaching your writing career, anyway: be original ... and a bit daring.

First, let's go over the usual 'Must-do' rules, because they are essential to improving your chances.

Word count. If 1,500 words is the max, don't send in a bulging epic.

Theme. If the rules indicate lambs gambolling through a sun-lit meadow, a blood-soaked gore-fest about Vlad the Impaler won't cut it.

Characters. Some competitions will suggest the central character, such as a librarian or someone's favourite aunt. Ignoring this and going off on one about a cat who is really a human in a fur coat is a sure-fire way of getting a rejection, no matter how clever the story.

Setting or time-frame. Ignoring the requirement for the story to be set in the 1930s, for example, or in a shopping centre, will ensure the return envelope gains instant use.

Deadline. This means not sending in your entry <u>after</u> the date specified. Before, yes; quite a long time before, even better, as early submissions help the judges with the reading process. And I hate to break this bit, but craftily sending in your entry so it plops onto the mat on the final morning, thus ensuring yours is read *last*, is not a guarantee of winning.

Entry fee. Not enclosing the fee but suggesting they take it out of your winnings doesn't work. Very confident, maybe, but no peanut. Competition organisers like to cover their costs, and sending a winner an IOU has never caught on.

Presentation and layout. Fewer and fewer comps now accept hand-written manuscripts. And among those insisting on printed pages, few appreciate eye-popping fonts, migraine-inducing print colours or penguins tripping around the margins to catch the eye of the judges.

Entry form and SAE. If specified, they're part of the rules. Lack of either will not improve your chances.

Now we come to the idea; the actual story. How on earth, bearing in mind your entry may be one of hundreds – maybe thousands these days, especially with internet announcements – can you come up with a winner, or an idea which will get your story plucked out of the pile among so many?

Well, one way is to consider it from the judges' perspective.

Take this example: imagine you are a judge in a Cute Cat Competition. You've seen endless moggies of every shape and hue scuttle and slink before your eyes; you've seen cute followed by cuter and are fast becoming immune to the endless stream of downright bloody cuteness. Four legs, tail, whiskers … so what?

How would *you* feel if all you saw coming down the cat-walk (sorry) was a further endless collection of cat cuties? Jaded, perhaps?

While writing judges have content rather than appearance to consider, the one thing they share is that they are all on the lookout for something different. That indefinable *it* which will cut through their jadedness and make them look twice.

Let us assume you've been set a theme of, say, jealousy. The setting is in a pub. Cue endless stories of dire and jealous doings among the beer kegs, glowering looks of anger and the judicious use of well-thrown darts from outside the oche.

It's a fairly safe bet that given these parameters, a large proportion of entries will be fairly similar in tone. So the thing to do is write something that will make the judges sit up and take notice. Sadly, eloquent prose and brilliant narrative may not be enough. What you have to do is sock 'em in the eye with something they don't expect. To go back to the earlier analogy, bring on a cat that is so darned <u>different</u> in its cuteness, they simply have to take notice. In this case, you could either burn the pub down, have it raided by the Drugs Squad or besieged by a three-day blizzard – anything which will lift the story out of the mundane and catch someone's attention.

Remember, this isn't the same as writing for magazines, where you are constrained by the magazine's house style and readership tastes. And open competitions are exactly that – open. So why not let your imagination really fly? Experiment a little; try something you've always wanted to, but never had a market for. Try a different voice. Be prepared to write outside your usual boundaries. If the setting allows, shock your audience – the judges – right out of their socks (but without being offensive, of course).

After all, there are lots of competitions and you are a writer. As Del Boy famously said: 'He who dares, Rodney … '

TOP TIPS

- Writing competitions are great testing grounds for focusing on deadline, theme and word count.

- Open themes allow writers to submit work difficult to place elsewhere.

- Some prize money is equivalent to market rates.

- Being a winner or even short-listed adds to your writing credentials.

Quality Control

JUST LIKE ANY PRODUCTION line, if an action is performed often enough, strange stuff can happen. In the white heat of the moment, mistakes and sloppy attitudes can creep in. It's not intentional, but all writers are human.

It's therefore worth making the occasional check on what you turn out, quite separate from the editing process, to avoid problems later on ... like when the editor might have said *yes* instead of *no*.

Value for money

I WAS ONCE ASKED by a writing course delegate how I knew whether I'd done a proper job of writing a story, and were there any specific steps to go through each time.

Well, not every writer follows the same approach to their craft, in the same way that not every builder takes the same steps to complete a project (and we all know how widely that can vary!) But there are some basic rules to follow which allow a certain elasticity in approach, depending on one's view of being a writer.

The first – and probably the main area – is telling a *complete* story. You can have the most beautifully worded tale in the world, with elegant narrative, realistic dialogue and mind-blowing descriptions of place, character and setting; but if your tale isn't rounded and complete, you haven't accomplished the main part of your job.

As writers, it is easy for us to get caught up in the mechanics of writing – the structure, grammar, punctuation and so forth – and to forget about the main components of a story. These should consist of, for the most part, a beginning, a middle and an end. The balance and importance of each of these may vary according to style, but as long as they are there in some form, the job has been done.

Imagine an ancient travelling minstrel, who sits down in the village square to regale the local peasants with a breathtaking tale of heroism, derring-do and romance. Instead of introducing the audience to his characters and saying how they fit into his tale, he launches straight in at the deep end. While he's talking, of course, people are looking at each other in puzzlement because he hasn't prepared the ground in the right way. Basically, he's dropped his characters into the frame like a bucket of bricks, and left it to the audience to do all the work. Naturally, because they're busy wondering what he's talking about, they miss further salient bits of the story. I find this happens occasionally, when I have to keep turning back a few pages of a book to find out what in the name of Moses is going on, and where did such-and-such a character spring from.

The same minstrel may well begin his story in the correct way, with a great opening line, proper introductions and a thrilling background setting. Unfortunately, he goes off the boil by careering straight towards the ending like a runaway hay cart, without any kind of build-up. This leaves the audience feeling short-changed, as if there's something missing. It's a bit like going from the starter straight to the pudding – sometimes fun but not always filling.

Our wandering minstrel might, on the other hand, build the tension and excitement, gradually drawing his audience into the story right from the opening, leading them towards what promises to be a gut-busting grand finale. Then, just as the end seems in sight, he promptly hikes up his breeches and walks away without finishing, leaving everyone with their jaws in the fly-catching position.

Cue revolting peasants, wondering what happened to the pay-off. And revolting peasants being what they are, the minstrel's next public appearance is likely to be centre-stage at the local rotten fruit-throwing gala.

The majority of readers like to finish a story with a feeling that they've been taken on a journey; that they've been entertained, shown some sights and brought to the end with a sense of satisfaction or conclusion. They may have a few questions, but these are usually along the 'what if …' lines, where their own imagination takes them off beyond the parameters set down by the author.

Where we writers might also fall down is in leaving gaps in the narrative, causing confusion by not being clear in what we are saying, or worse, not tying up loose ends. This is where editing is all-important, because we owe it to the reader to make as professional a job as possible of what we're doing.

It's a bit like looking at a graph: there will be peaks and troughs, reflecting the highs and lows of a story (activity versus descriptive narrative, for example). But as long as you have plenty of peaks, and they out-number the troughs, you can carry the reader forward into that much-described 'page-turning' territory, making them anticipate the next page for the thrills and excitement ahead.

TOP TIPS

- Is what you have written clear to the reader? Clarity is fundamental, in detail and plot. Lose clarity and you'll lose your reader.

- Have you explained who the characters are? It doesn't have to be a whole page, as long as you let everyone know where they came from and what part they play in your story.

- Have you left out or fudged what happened to character X or Y? If so, you may, like the minstrel, get more than just your five portions of fruit and veg. Readers fasten on to even minor characters, so you owe it to them to wrap up the detail.

- Have you brought the story to a satisfactory conclusion? *You* may know what the ending is, but have you made it clear to your readers, or will they be left forever wondering?

Quality Control (continued)

Getting your facts right

A WELL-KNOWN AMERICAN author, when asked how he knew so much about the innermost workings of the US Government, replied, 'I don't – I make stuff up.'

This isn't new, of course, and lots of writers spend their time making stuff up and doing it very well indeed. I have done it myself on more than one occasion, albeit not here. But then, I also write fiction, so I'm allowed.

However, those in what might be termed as the more grounded business of non-fiction writing, be it biography, travel, business, personal health and development – you name it, there's a subject that's been written about – should at least try to start from the basis of sticking to the facts. And, in terms of detail, it's not a bad habit for fiction writers to get into as well.

And why? Because someone, somewhere, will tell you about it if you don't.

Now I know there have been examples recently where this very basic rule has been breached – OK, let's not beat about the bush; blown out of the water – but let's begin from the standpoint that if you want to be a non-fiction writer ... it's the fiction part you should leave out. That way, we all know where we stand.

Having established that, it automatically means that making assumptions is also a big no-no. Whether assuming that point X lies a specific distance from point Y (and it doesn't) or that a subject's name is Bill (and it isn't), or that Z building was erected in 1300ad (and it wasn't), taking a stab at some detail simply because you can't be bothered to check, or because someone once told you it was so, is only a short hop from abandoning all sense of ethics and making stuff up altogether.

Does it really matter if you get a slight creep in detail this way? What's a few miles in the travel piece you've written? What if an ancient building you've written about actually dates from a hundred years *later*? What if someone you've done a piece about, and whom you've put on record as having been somewhere/done something/said something ... hasn't? Will the earth stop revolving because of any of these?

Well, hardly. But to most people – and certainly most editors (I leave out certain newspaper editors because they appear to operate on a different plane to the rest of us) – getting the facts right is not only applauded, but downright expected. It's essential, too, if you as a writer wish to be taken seriously.

It's said that you cannot libel the dead. Maybe. But you can still make a jolly good fist of upsetting their living relatives. And why print lies or distortions when the truth is (a) usually much more interesting and (b) so easily verified if only you put your mind to it?

A common criticism of a certain online encyclopaedia which is built, amended and used by anyone who cares to contribute, is that its very size and openness leaves it vulnerable to inaccuracy, bias or plain mischief. The debate goes on (I checked), but at least many readers are aware of the fact and tread cautiously.

Ever since the first word was written down, people have been happy to believe what they read rather than what they hear. One might argue that this is simplistic, but most of us do it every day when we pick up a newspaper (OK, not every newspaper – especially not those with short words, big letters and lots of pictures, but you know the ones I mean). It's a normal human instinct to believe what we read, mostly because the first people to write stuff down were regarded as educated ... and therefore probably in the know about stuff that nobody else had access to.

My, how things have changed.

Now, they're still educated, but they also play with the facts to suit themselves, whether through a hidden agenda or laziness, or – even worse – a contempt for their readers.

As a writer, there are few things more upsetting than being

told you've got your facts wrong. A rejection letter comes close in the bowel-shrivelling department, but let's pretend we're past that. It could be a simple mistake, which we can all make. It could be that you've been misinformed by someone you regarded as a reliable source. It could be that you didn't think it worth verifying.

Either way, it makes sense if you wish to be considered a professional writer, to make it an instinctive part of your day to check and re-check your facts. This includes things like spelling (especially of a subject's name, as no one likes to see their name wrong in print); dates (history buffs abound out there); locations (map readers ditto – and some satnav systems seem bent on leading drivers astray); directions (essential for travel or activity pieces, where your readership is being encouraged to visit somewhere of interest); and statistics (already open to wilful misinterpretation on an epic scale, there's always another person out there ready to challenge a figure – any figure – so the least you can do is give them little room to manoeuvre).

Finally, busy editors automatically warm to writers they have learned to trust. This means they will give you more work and your reputation will spread.

Can a writer ask more than that?

TOP TIPS

- Always check your facts. If in doubt – ask.

- Confirm details through more than one source.

- If not verifiable, either say so or leave it out.

- Never underestimate your readers.

- Take pride in getting it right.

- A good reputation brings its own rewards.

Keep 'em hooked

CHECK ALMOST ANY BOOK review, and it won't be long before you see such-and-such a book described as 'a real page-turner'. For the uninitiated, all it means is that the story races along in such a way that the reader cannot wait to ... well, you get the idea. There are plenty of other terms used by publicists and marketing people, such as 'a roller-coaster of a read' or even the very inventive 'unputdownable', but let us stick to page-turning as being a more explicit aim to keep our intended readers hooked.

That, after all, is what good writing is supposed to do, whether aimed at children reading the latest issue of a comic or older readers stretching out with their favourite author (or even, dare I suggest, a complete unknown on whom they've taken a punt just to see if he or she is worth pursuing). A sense of pace is certainly what I look for in a read, and I cannot recall deliberately sitting down to read something I knew would be the *opposite* to a page-turner since I was at school.

However, the page-turner expression is all very well when thinking of a book-length work, especially in thrillers or crime novels, where you can litter the pages with exciting events intended to draw the reader on to find out what happens next. In the same way, similar 'cliff-hanger' points in a book usually occur at the end of a chapter, the whole idea being that, instead of turning off the light and going to sleep, thereby waking up bright-eyed and bushy-tailed the following morning, the excited reader ploughs on regardless into the small hours (and wakes up feeling like a corpse but, one hopes, pleased with what he's read and anxious to read more).

But what about short stories in magazines, where the page layout is very different and usually in narrow columns? Here, if you wait too long before introducing some excitement, it may be too late.

The answer is to look carefully at how you pace your story. In a book-length work, you have a larger canvas where you can space out the tension versus the less dramatic sections (the rises and falls, if you wish) more easily. The short story is an entirely different animal. The rises are what hook readers into the suspension of everything else in life because they can't wait to see what happens next. Pots boil over, children wait for their tea, the lawn goes un-mown and Granny waits at the bus-stop. The falls can be equated to the in-between bits such as back-story, the build-up prior to a big scene, the descriptive narrative and sometimes, dialogue – although many writers use dialogue to bring tension to a story without relying on any wham-bam action scenes.

While it can sometimes be a problem over-loading your story with drama and conflict (and not everybody wants to be sitting breathlessly on the edge of their seat all the time), a far bigger problem, especially in short pieces, is to allow your story to wallow for too long in descriptive or simply uneventful fluff. The whole point of storytelling is that something must happen; your characters must experience something, and the best way of showing this is through action or emotional change.

Working on a sheet of A4 with anything up to fifteen words per line, it's easy to lose sight of the balance between the dramatic bits and the quieter sections. If using a PC, one way to overcome this when typing up your work is to highlight the page, select FORMAT, then COLUMNS, and choose say, three columns similar to a magazine page. Once you see your original page or so of dialogue appearing in a set of narrow columns, each containing no more than five or six words a line instead of fifteen, you might find that the reader has to go right to the bottom of the page before anything happens. In other words, you're a little heavy on the inaction.

If you don't have the facility to lay out your work in columns, the simplest answer is to look at the amount of descriptive narrative you've used. In itself, this is a good exercise, because we all tend to go 'off on one' occasionally, concentrating too much on describing how the birds are singing in the trees. Well, to hell with the birds – what about some action or a damned good row to liven things up a bit? Far more interesting and surely the point of the story.

If your story is more dialogue-led, with all the tension and conflict appearing between two or more characters, there's a danger in having too much dialogue without any intervening action. But this doesn't have to be violent or over-dramatised. In real life, we rarely talk without moving, nodding, kicking the furniture, gesticulating, eating, drinking and so on. Try breaking up your dialogue with some movement or expression on the part of the characters, and it lends a more unpredictable flow to your story. This is a relief for the reader, as well as avoiding some of the 'he said/she said' repetition we all fall into. It should also break up your paragraphs and avoid solid chunks of text filling the page, which can be heavy going and where you might – horror of horrors – lose your reader.

TOP TIPS

- End each chapter in a way that will make the reader want to turn the page.

- Cut out unnecessary descriptions in favour of action.

- Keep your characters moving around to raise the drama.

- Keeping sentences short and punchy improves the pace for the reader.

Quality Control (continued)

Keep it simple

I RECENTLY READ AN on-line review of a novel which fairly thudded with capital letters along the lines of 'A story of Deceit, Treachery and Betrayal, of Love Turned Sour, and the Search for Identity and Self-Discovery Amid Danger, Loss and … '

Actually, I can't remember the rest, because I was overwhelmed by an army of emoticons, those little animated creations for all occasions, which burst out of my computer and bounced around the room, screaming for attention.

At least, that's what it felt like.

If we follow the blurb on the back of book covers, many novels encompass all these themes and more. They paint lurid pictures designed to draw in the potential reader, using catchy words to appeal to the senses so that the customer parts with their hard-earned cash in return for a few hours of somebody else's pain, suffering, excitement, love and confusion.

Which is what they are supposed to do. This is the kind of stuff we as readers are looking for when we enter a bookshop. Equally, it's the kind of thing we as *writers* feed on as an indicator when we're looking for that brilliant idea which will propel us into the best-seller lists ahead of Dan Brown. If *this* is what's selling, we tell ourselves confidently, then we can do it, too. (Forgetting that 'this' was probably written over two years ago and something else is about to come into fashion.)

However, before we all go off and start bashing the keyboard into submission (excuse the pun) over *our* version of life in the fictional fast lane, it's worth drawing attention to the distinction between describing a published novel (the book reviews and the blurb on the cover) and sitting at the keyboard considering what will appeal to an agent or publisher about an idea that is still a glimmer in the writer's eye.

I'm not saying that an agent may not be turned on by a tantalising collection of buzz words like danger, love, disaster, treachery and so forth; many are and will continue to be, Lord bless 'em. However, looking at it from the writer's viewpoint, trying to pig out and include all these and more in your initial ideas for the novel may be a trifle unrealistic.

Keep It Simple is a useful credo to follow in most things. Ask any craftsman or manufacturer, and they will tell you that complex means time-consuming, challenging and usually a headache. Any sales person will tell you that making a presentation and including every single dot, comma and feature of your product up front, will invariably lose the customer before the halfway mark.

So it is with writers who set out right from the start to include in their novel a vast array of plotlines, devices and emotions, on the basis that if current novels in the bookshops have them, then so should *their* story. Some can do this; most can't.

Film studios and agents like to use very brief pitches when considering ideas for films (based, it is said, on the length of a lift (elevator) journey or the time it takes to chase a studio executive across a pavement). A pitch, for the *Lord of the Rings* trilogy, for example, might have been: 'Courageous elves, hobbits and humans wage ferocious battle against the forces of evil to save Middle Earth.' A bit succinct, perhaps, but that might have appealed to the studio execs. (One wonders if adding 'trees that walk and talk' would have had the same result?)

However, what actually went into the films came later, with the story of evil, jealousy, great courage and redemption, of family, death and almost unimaginable dark forces, all being built and layered into the script and bringing in the various elements which made the films the stonking success they were.

Set out to include too many elements in a story right from the very beginning, and you're likely to blow a gasket. It's like grabbing all the parts of a flat-pack of furniture and trying to assemble them at once. (I should know – I've assembled a few).

Equally, trying to deliberately bring in 'treachery', 'betrayal' or a host of other buzz words, purely because it sounds punchy and attention-grabbing, is certain to make the going hard. Far better to let your story – and the elements that drive it – evolve at their own pace. Sure, you need a plan or synopsis or some headings in mind, even if only in the form of key words as a way of giving the story direction. But allowing them to happen in an almost organic way is far easier.

In fact, many writers will testify to the fact that once they begin a story, they find it growing almost of its own volition, to the extent that some of the characters will take on actions and attitudes they hadn't planned. Equally, other characters will introduce themselves (and therefore additional plotlines) almost by force of personality. This might mean throwing the synopsis or plan out of the window, but nobody said you had to stick to it come hell or high water. It's your plan, after all; if you want to change it, go right ahead.

TOP TIPS

- Let the pace of the story do the selling.

- Don't go overboard with buzz words and hyperbole.

- Keep it simple – don't over-elaborate right from the start.

- Build to a crescendo, so the readers have something to look forward to.

Quality Control (continued)

Keep it real (Pt 1)

Put those leaves back on the tree!

I'M PARAPHRASING SLIGHTLY HERE, but that is the nub of what an editor once scrawled across one of my page proofs. The reason for this odd instruction was that I had somehow managed, during the course of one chapter, to take the season forward to full-blown winter when it should still have been late summer.

I'm not sure why I suddenly had bare trees or spindly, wind-blasted branches or whatever it was I had described out of context. Perhaps I had got distracted by atmosphere into thinking cold instead of warm. But from a day heavy with the last gasps of summer, suddenly I was wittering on about skeletal tree-tops with every leaf on the ground, fast turning into Mother Nature's compost.

Easy to do, of course, in the white heat of writing. But think what confusion the readers would have suffered if my editor hadn't been so quick to spot the mistake.

And it's just as easy to make slips like this in short fiction as in longer projects. One minute you have your characters in a morning setting, say, meeting after breakfast. The next minute they are enjoying a leisurely lunch – while apparently going through the same conversation – and your faithful reader is wondering whether the last couple of hours disappeared down some kind of literary black hole. Imagine that situation scaled up to reflect a whole day gone, or even two days, and you will fast lose your reader's attention and your own credibility as a writer.

But similar errors can creep in the other way, where time actually becomes too short for the scenes you are describing. Imagine, for example, that your plot requires a journey across a real and recognisable landscape (recognisable to your readers, that is). Ten to one someone out there will know the route you are describing intimately, probably because he follows it regularly and knows every bump, rut and pothole. Equally, he will know to the last second how long it takes to get from your A to B, yet here is your hero or heroine, blithely pootling along in half the time. Result: one unconvinced reader who might not come back for more.

So, how to keep things real and not wander off your timeline?

Well, the simplest way is to use a diary and make your events and settings as real as you can.

I find the best model to use is the large A4 format. You can find out-of-date ones, often on sale in office supply shops. These are useful because they have ample space for making plot notes, jotting down other pertinent details or holding those back-of-envelope scribblings for which we writers are famous.

For example, if your story is set over a number of days, then you should mark any points in the diary where you might need to mention something that will stand out because of the time of day. These might be related to refuse collections, postal deliveries, news broadcasts, opening/closing times, flight departures – anything which paints a picture of normality, and therefore requiring accuracy. If your character has to collect children from school, and this is essential to your story, then you should note this because it usually happens at a specific time. Thus, treat your timeline diary just as if it were your life unfolding, allowing the passing of time to be related to what you (or, in this case, your characters) are doing. Even if your storyline runs through the night, it is just as important, because while there won't be the same busy activity as in daytime, there will be plenty of atmosphere which will enhance the description of your scenes.

Now you have the time-related details covered, you can also happily dispose of other minor, but important items. The time of day, for example, will automatically impose certain references to temperature, light and, depending on season, atmospheric conditions, which could be useful or even necessary to your story. Following the diary will allow you to bring in helpful references to things like darkness, dawn, morning fog, street lights, vehicle headlights, shadow and even the position of the sun (having your hero gazing stoically into the early morning sun while facing west, for example, would be a bit of a let-down).

Making notes of these in your diary in advance will free you of the need to worry about them and allow you to concentrate on the main direction of your story. You can then scoop up the necessary background details when you arrive at that diary point, slotting them into place and thereby giving a more natural feel to your narrative.

The diary can be just as helpful on a far smaller scale, say, if your story is over hours rather than days. Time should still be seen to pass realistically, but you can work the diary to reflect hours instead of days, thus allowing you to keep a careful watch on those important minutes ticking away. All too often I have read scenes where two characters have passed a good half hour or so while waiting for something dramatic to occur, yet the on-going (and presumably continuous) dialogue between them suggests they have actually said very little.

Such timeline errors, while not always critical, can spoil the enjoyment of a story if not carefully monitored and plotted.

TOP TIPS

- Keep details of places, events and background consistent throughout your story.

- Use a diary to plot the timeline and keep track of what happens and when.

- Note the weather and atmosphere – often key to a plot.

- A diary helps you keep it real – and this will come across to the reader.

Keep it real (Pt 2)

ALONG WITH KEEPING A firm track of time in our stories, there
are a number of other areas where a moment's inattention can
let us down, and none more so than when it comes to small
points of detail like colour and distance.

Taking colour first, it is easier than you might think to slip
from a character having brown eyes to suddenly having blue
ones. Or from being fair-haired to sandy. Not earth-shattering,
you might think, on the grand scale of things. But consider the
readers. From the moment they begin your story, they
inevitably start to construct a mental picture of what character A
or B looks like. Even if you haven't littered the page with
specific details, the image still appears, because that is the
nature of the human brain; it cannot deal with blanks, so will fill
in the spaces, taking clues from the speech, emotions or
mannerisms you as the writer have assigned your characters.

You can test this by speaking to anyone who has seen a film
of a well-known book. Ten to one people will say that the
screen persona didn't resemble their idea of X in the slightest.
You might be of the same opinion … but for entirely different
reasons, because you will have constructed your own image of
X, using your own interpretation of the author's clues.

As writers, we have to consider the danger of finding that,
after several pages of having portrayed the central character as a
Brad Pitt look-alike, so that all the reader has to do is read the
name to instantly picture the face, our descriptions might
suddenly vary sufficiently to portray him with more of the look
of a Keanu Reeves.

A way out of this dilemma is to use a real photo as your
model. I don't mean a shot of Brad Pitt, necessarily, but try
using a cutting from a magazine, which matches as closely and

as realistically as possible the kind of face you want your character to have. Keep it handy and you can, whenever you need to, quickly check to see if those eyes are meant to be blue or hazel, the nose broken or straight, or if the character originally had hair parted left or right (or, indeed, had any hair at all). The larger the picture, the more detail you can mention – if appropriate – such as laughter lines, cheekbone definition and so forth.

Height is another factor to keep an eye on. If one of your characters is described as being somewhat vertically challenged, there will be certain things he or she cannot do easily, such as reaching casually up to wipe a cobweb from the ceiling or pluck a suitcase from the top of a wardrobe. And as for that pastime of many commuters, strap-hanging on the London underground in rush-hour, well, forget it unless you want them swinging like a side of beef all the way from Liverpool Street to Paddington.

I remember reading in one novel some years ago where a 'stocky, bow-legged' character entered one end of a billiard room, covering the distance to the other end in 'three slow, purposeful strides'. Well, if he did, he must have had very unusual legs or was using stilts – something the writer plainly forgot to mention.

Physical ability and fitness are other potential pitfalls. Running up a long flight of steps without effort is reasonably simple for someone of above average fitness. To most of us, this might at the very least make us slightly short of breath. Yet some characters, described as being average, in humdrum jobs and with no obvious signs of following any kind of fitness regime, are shown suddenly completing what amount to stunning feats of stamina with cool aplomb … and even pausing to light a fag afterwards!

Another character recently was described as drinking large quantities of water. Bottles, mugs, cups, glasses – every few pages had him gulping down copious amounts of God's ale, but without any mention of that equally mundane but essential (you would have thought) activity of getting rid of it.

Seasonal information is a sure-fire bear trap waiting for the unwary. Like my own slip-up with the trees, to describe summer flowers blooming when they should be dead and withered, is to invite incredulity. Certain species of wildlife, especially birds, while tempting to drop into the scenery for a touch of atmosphere, might not, for reasons of hibernation or migration, be around at the time – global warming or not.

The simple way around all this is to keep unnecessary details to the minimum. In any case, short stories rarely offer the space to go into lengthy descriptions, so paring these down is a useful discipline to develop. As long as the pace whizzes along and keeps the reader entranced, the absence of too many references to tics, moles, gammy legs, stray dogs, passing wildebeest and so forth won't be missed. Venturing into longer works, however, where there is both space and the need to go into greater detail, and even the seasoned writer's attention can start to wander. The result? Those leaves fall from the trees when they should still be attached, eyes twinkle with a different colour and seasoned couch-potatoes perform amazing feats of agility, when all the while they should be on their knees gasping for breath, instead of calmly sucking on a congratulatory fag.

TOP TIPS

- Help the reader by being consistent with descriptions of characters; eyes, hair, height, etc., should remain constant.

- Too much unnecessary detail can confuse the reader and makes writing more difficult than it needs be.

- Allow the reader to fill in a few blanks; each one will have his or her own vision of characters and place.

Editing

EDITING YOUR WORK IS simply another chance to review and tidy up what you have written. To correct typos, re-phrase, amend and improve, to make your work tighter and leaner, to cut out superfluous words or to flesh out what may appear unclear.

Use the editing process to satisfy yourself that you have written the best work you can, whether a short story, article or full-length book. Too many mistakes and even the most obliging editor will decide not to proceed further.

Editing (continued)

When less is more

MY OLD ENGLISH MASTER, known irreverently as 'Drac' Hall ('Drac' for Dracula, because of a severe widow's peak, slicked back hair and a cadaverous smile), must have possessed the soul of a journalist. A brilliant, no-nonsense teacher, he managed to make what many saw as a bone-dry subject both interesting and challenging – at least to me. And one of those ways was by introducing us early to the idea of editing our writing.

Onc of the more regular gauntlets hurled to the floor before us was to get an unwilling class to précis its work – or more interestingly – to précis passages from published authors. Most of my classmates hated this exercise with a venom, and would rather have held their bare wrists over a Bunsen burner or gone through a double lesson in history. I loved it because I could usually see immediately where some economies of words could be made, just as I found out in later life that accountants and business people can spot anomalies when reading a balance sheet.

I admit I don't always manage to practise what Drac preached, although the instinct is always there. Indeed, his teaching has come in useful over the years, and never more so than in the editing process, when I find I may have got carried away and over-written a piece which needs cutting back, sometimes severely.

The dictionary meaning of the word 'précis' is given as a 'summary or abstract of a text'. But the way Drac taught it was to make it an everyday tool, cutting out each unnecessary word without taking away the meaning or drama of the whole. The way he did it was to give us a text – say, half a page – and count the words. We then had to read it two or three times before going through and culling every word we felt wasn't absolutely

225

vital.

Alongside all the maths and science geeks, who reigned supreme in *their* sphere, this was my chance to shine – and I thoroughly enjoyed it. And that enjoyment has remained with me ever since. A thousand words too many? No problem. A hundred over the top? Easy.

Where it gets really challenging is when aiming for a short story of, say, 1,500 words, only to end up with 1,700. That 200-word excess is a large percentage of the overall amount, and can be devilish to prune away without some serious soul-searching. But if that's what the editor demands, that's what you have to do. Otherwise, no peanut.

Translate that to a book-length manuscript, where you may have written 100,000 words but the editor only wants 90,000, and it really is a question of scale. But the task remains the same. Fail to cut back where required, and you stand a good chance of losing a possible sale.

A useful way of practising the art of précis for yourself is to take at random any paragraph from a novel (or magazine page) and see where you can pare it down. The aim is to retain the full sense of the whole passage without making it sound as though some important words are missing.

As an example, my last sentence could read: *The aim is to retain the sense of the passage without sounding as though some words are missing.*

Result: 23 words pared down to 18. Not a lot in one sentence, but practised over a complete manuscript, the scale of cuts soon mounts up.

This is a useful exercise to pursue as a regular part of our writing, because we can all be tempted into over-fluffing sentences with too many adjectives and descriptive prose, none of which necessarily enhances what we are trying to say. It's especially notable when tension is called for, and the tendency creeps in to go overboard with scenery or emotion at the expense of action and forward momentum.

Ideally, you need some distance to précis with any degree of objectivity. Trying to cull words during the writing is, I find, more likely to become an obstacle to finishing the chapter or story; far better to leave it for a day or two, then go back and read it through a couple of times to see what catches the eye.

Reading your work aloud can also help, as extraneous words will sometimes cause the tongue to trip. If this happens, either prune it or use a different word.

Mastering the skill of précis can be liberating, specially when working to strict word counts. Setting out with a specific number of words in mind can be a distraction, where the brain becomes all too aware of the target to be reached rather than the subject of the story. I concentrate on writing the story first, and worry about the word count afterwards.

True, experience gives me a rough idea of where I am, so I'm hardly likely to go too mad. But I'm never worried about having to cut back on my words. Thanks to Drac Hall, it's something I can do.

TOP TIPS:

- Ask yourself – is every word vital to the sentence?

- Can you cut any words without spoiling the overall effect or meaning?

- Can cutting words improve the flow of your text?

- Can punctuation take the place of a word or words?

- Does pruning increase or decrease the tension in your writing?

Editing (continued)

Stop fiddling!

A COMMON TOPIC OF conversation came up recently, when a lady asked me about a book she was writing. 'How do I know when it's finished?' she queried.

The cheeky answer would have been 'When you write END at the bottom of the final page'. However, while there's an obvious truth in that, I've heard the same point mentioned on several occasions, and found that the question usually arises for two very different reasons. Which of the two is causing the problem is where the individual writer has to decide.

The first comes out of the editing process. This encompasses everything from crossing all the 't's' and dotting the 'i's', through verifying facts to checking timelines and continuity of detail (the blue eyes suddenly turned brown, for example). Whether this is done during or after the main task of writing depends on individual preference. Some people like to edit as they go along, tidying up any mistakes or omissions at the end of each day; others prefer to TTBS (tell the bloomin' story) and get the bulk of the work done, leaving it until later to worry about the grind of editing, when they can don a different hat.

Personally, I find there is something to be said for the TTBS approach, since coming back to a chapter after an absence often gives me a new perspective on the content and layout when judged against the rest of the work. I believe this allows me to see the detail with a more dispassionate eye, and I tend not to spend as much time editing as I do when I take the do-it-as-I-go-along approach and end up fretting myself into a nervous wreck over dots, commas and doubtful phraseology.

Whichever way works for you is best. But where some writers trip up is simply in over-editing their work. This usually occurs where you find yourself drawn back to a specific paragraph or section of a story, altering the wording because you are not quite satisfied with what you have written. If this happens more often than is usual, you should give it to somebody you can trust and ask his opinion, on the basis that a fresh eye might see what you cannot.

Because we sometimes get too close to a story, and can't see the wood for the trees (apologies for that cliché), we begin to fiddle and pick away at the work until it risks becoming an obsession. The end result – other than never finishing what we started – is that we end up so far away from where we began, it no longer makes sense.

It's a bit like the DIY bodger who, trying to level a rickety dining table, saws off bits from each leg in turn, eventually ending up with everyone eating Japanese-style.

In general, you wouldn't have thought there would be too many problems with deciding how a sentence or paragraph should be set down on the paper. Yet occasionally, something about the appearance on the page can look odd, causing you to be dragged back time and time again without knowing why, and reaching for your fiddling pen.

It could be simply a matter of clumsy spacing, which can hide or interrupt the pace of your delivery. If you want to say something that has some impact for example, introducing a piece of information that, in a film would be accompanied by some dramatic *dum-dum-dum* music, don't bury it in a busy section of 'he said', 'she said' dialogue, where it will get lost or watered down. If it's important, then far better to have it out there by itself, where it gets noticed.

Your answer may simply be in revising the layout of the problem section. You may have, for example, character A confronting character B, with the all-important high point being where A places a truly damning document on the table. (Cue dramatic music). Yet for some reason the passage doesn't look right or command the weight you were looking for. The question is, have you put the information in the right place, or has it become little more than a vague gesture which your reader may not spot, thus losing the dramatic inference?

Try giving it some room, and alter the layout. Use the line

space to set the action apart from the dialogue, and it could make all the difference.

The second reason for fiddling is more a matter of confidence; many writers find it difficult at first to let their work go out into the big, wide world. This is a great shame, because if you want your work to be read – and published – you owe it to yourself to face this ultimate test. In a nutshell, it comes down to having the brass neck to say 'Enough' and to stick your pride and joy in an envelope and entrust it to whatever fate awaits it.

Thinking about it, why short-change yourself? While there are some who might prefer to hover in that writing limbo, where judgement is never passed on their work, most people would probably agree that the *not* knowing is more difficult to live with.

If you don't take this step, you'll never find out. For more on this, see the following chapter **'Submitting Your Work'**.

TOP TIPS

- Learn to know when you have done enough. Over-editing can be counter-productive.

- If it looks wrong, try re-writing a passage. Then move on. You can always come back later.

- Finish the story first, then read it through to gain a sense of the flow.

- Don't get hung up on one point. If you really don't like it, cut it out or replace it.

Editing (continued)

To cut a long story short

HAVE YOU EVER FACED the prospect of sitting down to a big meal, but settled for a bar of chocolate instead … and found it just as satisfying? I know I have – especially when I was single and feckless (as opposed to married and feckless) and 'balanced' and 'diet' were two words I tried to avoid using in the same sentence. Somehow, chocolate seemed infinitely more appealing than a helping of meat and two veg – and there was no washing up afterwards. (Come to think of it, apart from a health conscience, what's changed?)

I get the same feeling sometimes when choosing a book. Every now and then, the idea of wading into something which I know is going to be filling, satisfying – even enriching … is simply too heavy for the mood I'm in at the time. And that's when reaching for a magazine, with its bite-sized chunks and snazzy photos is so much easier, and ultimately does the job.

This leads on to taking the same approach to our writing, and rather than using a lengthy, drawn-out style, no matter how well-written it might be, an instant, snappier prose might be more appropriate.

Describing a character as having florid, jowly features, loose, fleshy lips and a permanent scowl is all very well, and paints a clear picture. But – depending on the mood and tone of your story, of course – you could achieve the same from saying that he looks like a bulldog chewing a wasp. The image this conjures up does the job, and describes the character's mood as well as his appearance.

Similarly, lengthy narrative about a grey winter's day, with much emphasis on dull colour tones, blustery winds and the feel of cold air on the skin, can and does work extremely well. But if your story doesn't demand that level of detail, why not settle for saying that the day sat like a grey blanket, cold and damp – then get on with the action?

This abbreviated form of description works especially well in short fiction, where every word must count and you can find yourself over-reaching the required total all too quickly, yet still with a lot of untold story to go. Cutting out unwanted adjectives and adverbs is fine, but sometimes that is not enough. You have to face the fact that you need to do some ruthless pruning.

Describing someone as angry, then writing after some dialogue, ' … she said angrily …' merely doubles up what you already know, and uses up part of your valuable word count. It's also irritating for the reader to be told something the author's previous words have already described quite clearly.

Equally, writing that someone is unable to stand upright due to intoxication, with additional detail about blood-shot eyes, sallow skin, mussed hair and the general slovenly appearance of someone who's been hitting the bottle is all fine and good. But wouldn't it be just as easy to say 'he was drunk'? Everyone knows what a drunk looks like, and unless you are describing specific actions which have a bearing on the story, further mention of swaying, blinking, belching, or any of the other disgusting things people do when sozzled, are superfluous. Where this economy of words can be most easily achieved is in the editing phase, when you pretty much know where the story is going – or has gone. Then you can look back over what you have written and judge where some words can come out without harming the flow of the story, and whether all you are doing is delaying getting to the point.

In an argument between two characters, for example, the scenery around them might be of little relevance to the action, unless they are arguing while struggling through a snow storm or baling out a sinking boat. Then you might have a need to drop in the occasional descriptive hint about gusting wind snatching their words away, or a surge of something nasty coming up through the bilges and interrupting a rant about who pulled out the plug thingy that let in the ocean. But most of your writing will concentrate on the characters, the direction and pace of their conflict and the emotion crackling in the air, not necessarily how they look.

In fast-moving stories, readers want to know what is happening now, where it will lead and what happens next. They want to be dragged forward relentlessly, eagerly anticipating the next piece of action, rather than being treated to well-written yet ultimately unnecessary chunks of prose which won't take them into that breathless imagery they are looking for. In the lead-up to the action, yes, there will be a need to paint a picture of the surroundings, to give readers a clear idea of where the scene is taking place. But there comes a point where they need to be rushed headlong into and through the action, and out the other side, otherwise they begin skimming (surely the worst thing writers can hear about their work, second only to the sound of it hitting the wastebasket.)

TOP TIPS

- Ask yourself: can I describe this scene in a shorter, punchier style?

- Are my words too flowery for the general storyline?

- Does this description add to my story in any way?

- Am I merely delaying the pace of the action?

Submitting Your Work

SURELY THE TOUGHEST TEST for most first-time writers: placing their work in an envelope and sending it off to some faceless unknown, where they imagine it will be ripped to shreds, used as paper planes or plagiarised (none of which happens – they're all too busy).

In fact, it should be one of the easiest things for any writer to do. After all, it's unlikely you will know the editor, or that he or she will know you from a bucket of sawdust. So where's the problem?

Write, edit, check and submit. It's the natural culmination of all your hard work.

Come on, you know you want to …

Submitting Your Work (continued)

The words wot I wrote

SOMETHING THAT MAY COME as a cold shower to first-time writers (and some older hands, too, along the way) is that the words you have sweated buckets over, those precious drops of prose, those glistening gems of magic that must surely put you in line for a major writing award, do not always appear on the published page in quite the way you imagined. Or, to use a thespian analogy, it's not unknown for your best moments to end up on the editorial version of the cutting-room floor.

Pause for a stiff drink and a lie-down while the horrid prospect of literary butchery goes away. *How can they do that to my baby? Is it allowed?*

The answers are, easily and yes. The reasons are varied, none of which you should take personally if you wish to grow as a writer. But you need to be aware of them before your outrage leads to a stiff letter to an offending editor.

Space in magazines is a constant battle. And in today's cost-conscious publishing business, there is inevitably some competition between content (the articles and stories) and revenue other than sales (i.e. advertising). It is a sad fact that for many magazines, the advertising income, which is often what keeps them afloat, may occasionally have to take precedence over a piece of content. This also explains why a piece sold some time ago has still not appeared in print.

The other reasons may be seasonal slant (there's not much call for a short story about Father Christmas in July, for example, or a feature about the joys of a weekend's sunny narrow-boating in December). It may also be because the editor has recently published a story with a similar theme and wants to hold off for a while before broaching the same subject again.

Timing apart, however, there are other reasons for editorial

237

changes.

The threat of litigation is one. We all know about racism and sexism, but making any old statement about real people or bodies (corporations, that is, not dead ones) which is blatantly untrue, is also discouraged. You should be wary of dragging into a fictional piece a real (living) person or corporation, purely to give your work a semblance of realism. Suggesting, for example, that some piece of villainy in a crime story involves a real corporation is very risky and an editor will be quick to spot this potential gaff. Equally, some editors are reluctant to give XY or Z company any free advertising, which is why suggesting your heroine munches her way through a variety of well-known snacks or chocolate bars or smokes a particular brand of cigarette will not always go down too well.

Editors are also less than keen on allowing factual errors or statements to appear within their pages. If they spot, for example, something blatantly incorrect in your story, they will either contact you to amend it, change it or simply leave it out altogether, because it is not only your name which will suffer, but more importantly the name and reputation of their magazine. As an example, for a war-time story I wrote some years ago, a magazine used an illustration of a gas-mask carried by the heroine – a member of the WAAF. They received several letters pointing out that the bag used would not have been carried by this person because it was the wrong branch of the services. We might consider this hair-splitting, but if it spoils the reader's enjoyment of the story and magazine, then it is worth the editor taking note. While the choice of illustration here was beyond my control, I learned one very valuable lesson: as a writer I should make sure I get *my* facts right, because if I don't, someone out there will notice!

Another reason for editorial change is that the editor knows the magazine and its market. He or she may love your submission, but they may feel that a few small touches here and there will make the tone or 'feel' of the article or story just a little more acceptable to the readers. This, after all, is what editors are for. If there were none (as sometimes seems the case with some publishing sites on the Internet), then we could all send in any old rubbish without concerning ourselves too much with punctuation, style, grammar or detail.

What some writers might also forget is that something blindingly obvious to them may not necessarily be so evident to the reader. In this case the editor may feel the need for some tweaking for clarity.

So, if your joy at seeing your work in print is momentarily soured by seeing changes in the prose, do not reach automatically for the bucket of vitriol. There may be a good reason for it. Anyway, a rant at the editor is a sure-fire way of losing the opportunity of future work being accepted.

TOP TIPS

- Ask yourself: is the content factually correct?

- Does it read smoothly?

- Does it suit the target magazine's tone and style?

- Are there any injurious or potentially libellous statements?

- Is there any padding, which an editor might be tempted to cut?

- If, after all this, there are still changes to your submission, accept them with good grace and move on to the next project.

Don't be shy

IT'S A FAIR BET that while many readers of these pages may be embarking on their first writing projects, an equally fair number will be virtual 'old hands', with a drawer/data stick/hard drive full of manuscripts.

But it's also safe to assume that the first group will share one thing in common with a surprising number of the second: they will never have actually submitted their work to a magazine editor.

The reasons for this can be varied, from the 'I'm not ready yet' to the 'I'm not interested in being published' (although I've never met a writer truly serious about the latter).

But, setting aside for a moment those who aren't ready right now (they *will* be one day), a surprising number of writers suffer from a problem they don't like to admit to: shyness.

A published writer I know once confessed that it took her years before she drummed up the courage to send out her very first submission. The reason she cited? She didn't think she was good enough. I've heard others – mostly in non-fiction writing – say that they didn't consider themselves knowledgeable enough on the subject, so why should a magazine editor even consider their work?

Fair comment. But, like going into the water for the very first time, you have to start somewhere. And while it might seem a big step, all it needs is that first deep breath and a healthy dollop of self-confidence in the fact that – unlike in water, at least – you won't actually sink like a brick.

Bear this one thought in mind: *the editor doesn't know you.* Now that may be stating the blindingly obvious, and is normally considered a disadvantage when pitching for work. But let's turn it on its head for this one instance, and use it. Also consider that that same editor receives many submissions each day, most of them unsolicited. As such, they are simply words on paper, showing varying degrees of professionalism and skill. Yours will stand or fall equally with the others.

The other factor to keep in mind is that editors aren't looking to reject work – quite the opposite. They *need* articles and/or stories – content – to put in their magazines. (Some may strive to give the opposite impression, but, believe me, they need words on the page like a celebrity needs a flash-bulb). Without content, they have only adverts, and advertisers are a notoriously picky bunch when it comes to paying for space in magazines without readers.

In this brash new world we inhabit, you, too, have a right to be heard. The only rider to this is that editors and readers have a right to be offered the very best that you can produce, so don't stint on presentation or effort – it does make a difference.

Your manuscript, whether short or long, fiction or fact, might be a potential winner. But festering away unseen in your sock drawer, it does nothing, achieves nothing and is only so much paper and ink. (Some 'writers' use this option to kid themselves that they've never had anything rejected. That's like saying you've never fallen off a bike because you've never actually tried to ride one!)

There is also the 'what if?' scenario. What if JK Rowling had thought her first work lacked magic? If Elton John's lyricist, Bernie Taupin, had thought his candle might go out in the wind? If John Sullivan had thought Del and Rodney Trotter were a couple of plonkers? If Quentin Tarantino had pulped his fiction?

Some writers claim they pursue their art solely for their own pleasure. So do many amateur painters, sculptors, musicians and potters. And while I would never decry this, how many of them would actually like to share that pleasure with others?

These same arguments apply, naturally, to non-fiction writing, but with an added factor: the question of authority; *do I have a right to put down my views, knowledge or observations on paper for others to read?*

Of course you do. It's how we all learn from others and,

providing you have researched, organised and verified your facts, and written the piece in an informative, entertaining – and above all – fresh way, who is to say your piece shouldn't be published?

Certainly an editor won't if the piece is well-written, timely and appropriate for the magazine in question.

TOP TIPS

- Make the submission as professional as you can. Even a first effort stands a better chance of being read if it is well presented.

- With non-fiction, highlight your knowledge of the subject rather than your lack of experience. A new, fresh take on a subject can often score where others fail.

- Take all comments as helpful (and use them), but remember that they are simply one person's opinion.

- The more you do it, the easier it gets – and the greater the desire to succeed!

- Whatever your writing genre, you'll never know if you *can* until you *do*.

- And finally, if required, enclose a stamped, addressed envelope every time.

Submitting Your Work (continued)

Rejection is just the beginning

DURING A CREATIVE WRITING class recently, a student bravely confided that she had received her very first rejection (of a short story submitted to a magazine). It was especially brave because another student had just announced her first sale.

Bearing in mind that rejection can be a traumatic disappointment to any writer, she was quite flummoxed when everyone clapped and offered their congratulations!

No, they weren't being unkind. In fact, most of her student colleagues were expressing justifiable admiration, because she had done what many of them had not: she had actually submitted a story for publication.

This comes back to one of the great – often unconsidered – hurdles for new writers: if you never submit anything, you will never know whether you have written something worthwhile. Instead, all you will have is the judgement of well-meaning friends or family, who either (a) pull their punches because they wish to be kind or (b) kick your legs out from under you because they wish to be 'honest'.

As has been covered here before, talking about being a writer is fine; thinking about it is good. But to *be* a writer, there's no substitute for simply getting down and doing it. It's no different to any other line of endeavour, such as saying 'I'd love to have an allotment and go green'. Unless you pick up your fork and start digging, all you are doing is fantasising about it.

In the same way, wanting to write and sell your work is never going to become a reality until you send your stories or articles out into the world to be considered by a professional.

So what are the reasons for this common dilemma?

Confidence. You may feel that you've written an absolute blinder of a story, with all the required buttons and bells, lots of beautifully drawn characters and a sizzling plot. But you just don't have that final surge of confidence required to boot the thing off the end of the branch and allow someone else to see whether it has merit. Well, you're not alone, believe me. Plenty of people find this a real struggle, and spend their days writing stories which go nowhere.

What a waste!

Remember this: you are sending your work out anonymously (or as good as), because the editor doesn't know you from a hole in the hedge, your name is just that – a name – and he/she will judge your writing on its merits rather than who you are, where you live or what you call yourself.

Quality. This is linked to confidence, but comes down more often to specific feelings of doubt about whether your story is *good* enough or will be laughed right into the bin. This is something only you can answer, but don't forget that all successful writers had to start somewhere. And every writer under the sun has been rejected at some stage.

Another point about being judged: some editors can spot a good story the moment they see it, but may still reject it for various reasons (got one like it already; wrong time of year; not a current topic; needs polishing, etc). If it's close enough, some editors will make a comment rather than simply sending it back. If so, take heed and take advantage of the fact that someone has noticed your work. And if there is a positive comment, the door is opening for you to try again!

Competition. This means, quite simply, that you subconsciously feel there must be lots of better writers out there whose work will blow yours out of the water and show it up for what it is.

Actually, not true. Yes, there are many talented writers around. But *your* envelope will fit through the same letterbox as theirs, will open just like theirs and will look the same on the page. In other words, you start on the same line as everyone else.

Focus. Are you unsure about who you are aiming at? If so, check your target market again and make an honest assessment about whether your work fits that market or should be sent somewhere more appropriate to the content. If it really doesn't fit, don't waste your time or theirs; look for another target.

Parameters. Are you sub-consciously aware that you have been a little 'elastic' with word count, content, characters or genre? It's easy to do when you're in the white heat of creating a story, and you may hate cutting something which you consider fundamental to the story. But the first thing to do is become absolutely comfortable and familiar with your target magazine's guidelines, so that when your story goes into the post, you are confident that it will meet their most basic requirements, rather than falling at the first fence.

If it still comes back, even though you've followed all the guidelines, take the opportunity to re-read the story and make an honest judgement about what might have caused the rejection. If you really cannot see anything wrong, send it somewhere else!

TOP TIPS

- Get it finished, get it right for the market and send it out.

- A 'no' from one editor isn't a rejection by the entire industry.

- Take rejection as an opportunity to re-read your story.

- Challenge yourself. Be daring and submit your work.

- You have an absolute right to try. Don't waste it.

Writers' Resources

WRITERS CANNOT WORK IN a vacuum. We all need information, advice, distraction and a view on how others do it. The following sites and organisations are not exhaustive, and do not cover the compete range of writing genres. However, they offer a wealth of detail and inspiration for writers, and will lead on to extra sources of help and opportunity. Take time out to smell the coffee … and see what's out there.

Writers' Magazines

Writer's News – www.writers-online.co.uk
Writing Magazine – www.writers-online.co.uk

Literary Agency (Novels)

DHH Literary Agency – www.dhhliteraryagency.com

Writers' Organisations, Societies & Groups

The Crime Writers' Association (CWA) – www.thecwa.co.uk
The Romantic Novelists' Association (RNA) – www.rna-uk.org
International Thriller Writers (ITW) – www.thrillerwriters.org
Mystery Women (MW) – www.mysterywomen.co.uk
Historical Novel Society – www.historicalnovelsociety.org
British Science Fiction Association – www.bsfa.co.uk
Horror Writers Association – www.horror.org
Science Fiction Writers Association – www.sfwa.org

Lending and Copyright

Authors Licensing & Collecting Society (ALCS) – www.alcs.co.uk
Public Lending Right (PLR) – www.plr.uk.com
Society of Authors – www.societyofauthors.org

Agents, Publishers and Markets

Writers' and Artists' Yearbook – www.writersandartists.co.uk
Writer's Market UK – www.writersmarket.co.uk

Useful Websites

The following are some sites the author has come across offering help and information to writers, whether through views, reviews, interviews, market information, publishing opportunities, connecting readers to writers or simply talking about writing. There is a bias towards crime and thrillers, but the premise is the same: read and absorb.
If they don't inspire you to get writing and submitting, nothing will!

Spike the Cat – www.spikethecat.co.uk and www.spikethecatltd.blogspot.com
Fiction is Stranger Than Fact – http://fictionisstrangerthan fact.blogspot.com
Morgen Bailey – www.morgenbailey.com
Writers' Services – www.writersservices.com
Womagwriter's blog – http://womagwriter.blogspot.com
The Crime of it All – www.thecrimeofitall.com
Shots Magazine – www.shotsmag.co.uk
Thrills Kills 'N Chills – http://thrillskillsnchills.blogspot.com
Crime Time – www.crimetime.co.uk
Book2Book – www.booktrade.info
Permission to kill – www.permissiontokill.com
Reviewing the Evidence – www.reviewingtheevidence.com
The Bookseller – www.thebookseller.com
Euro Crime – www.eurocrime.co.uk
Publishers Weekly – www.publishersweekly.com
Crime Squad – www.crimesquad.com
Fantasy Writers – www.fantasy-writers.org
Fantasy Factor – www.fantasy.fictionfactor.com